Petra Cortright

E-Girl

Hesse Press

Petra Cortright

E-Girl

Hesse Press

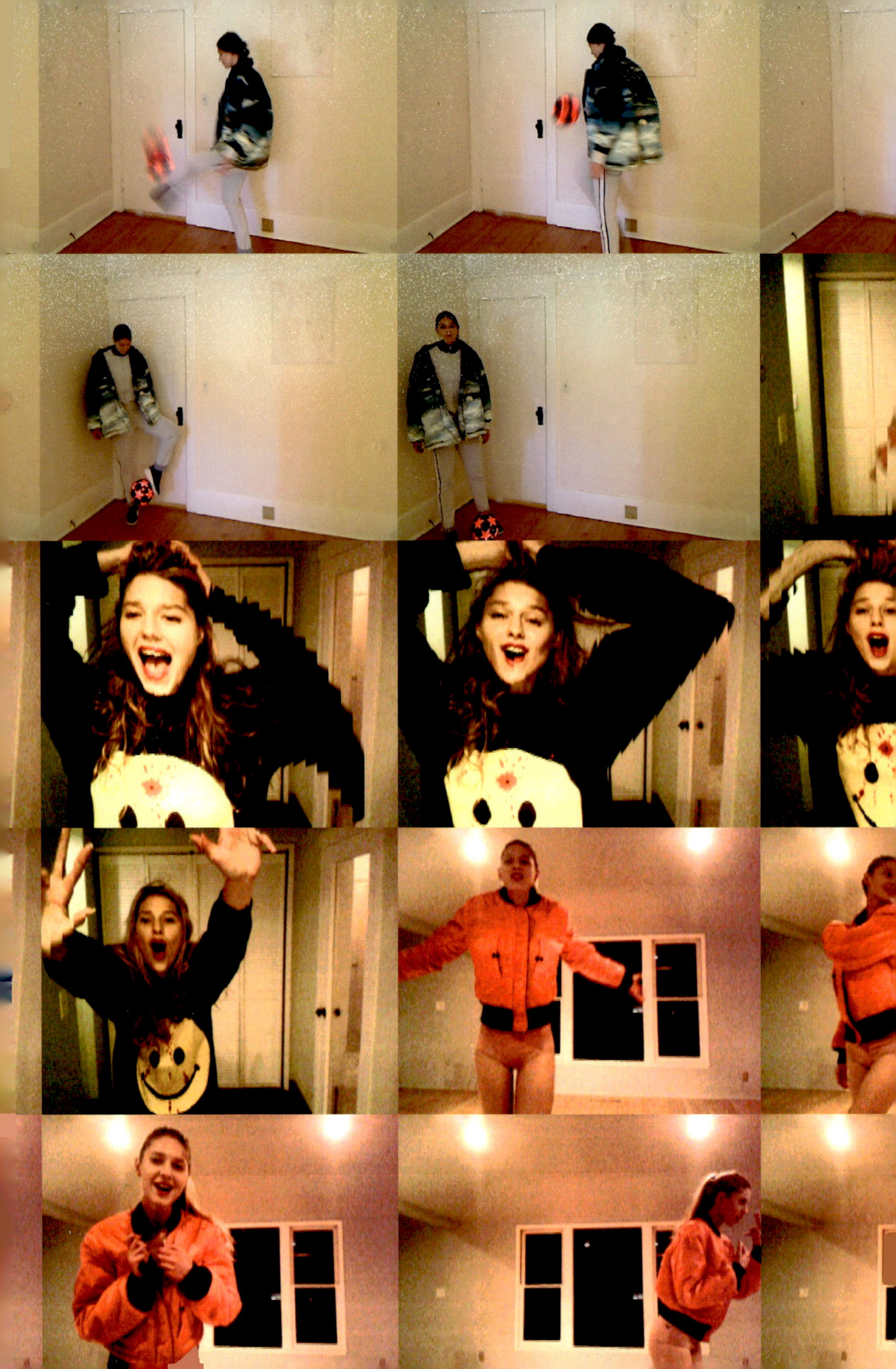

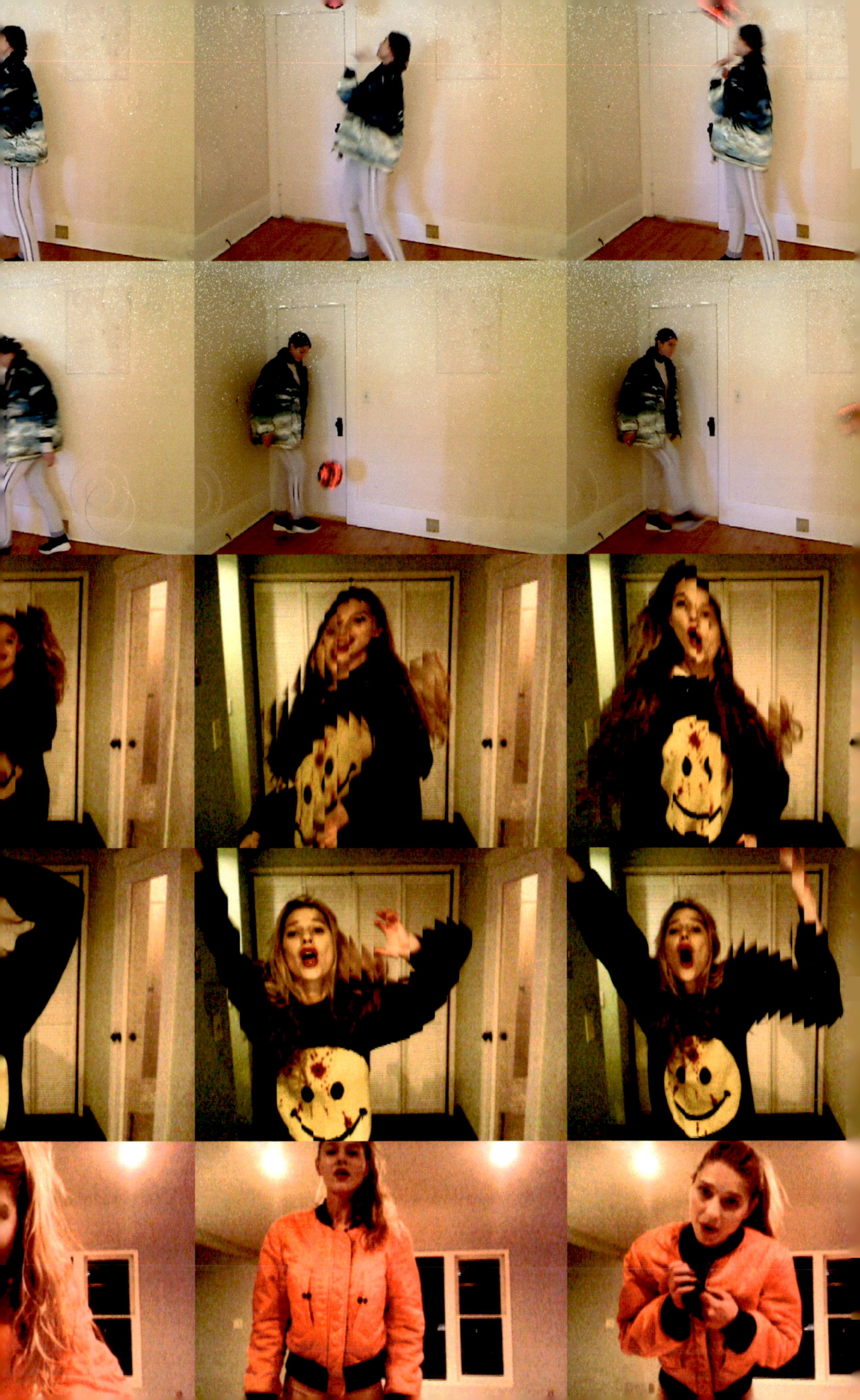

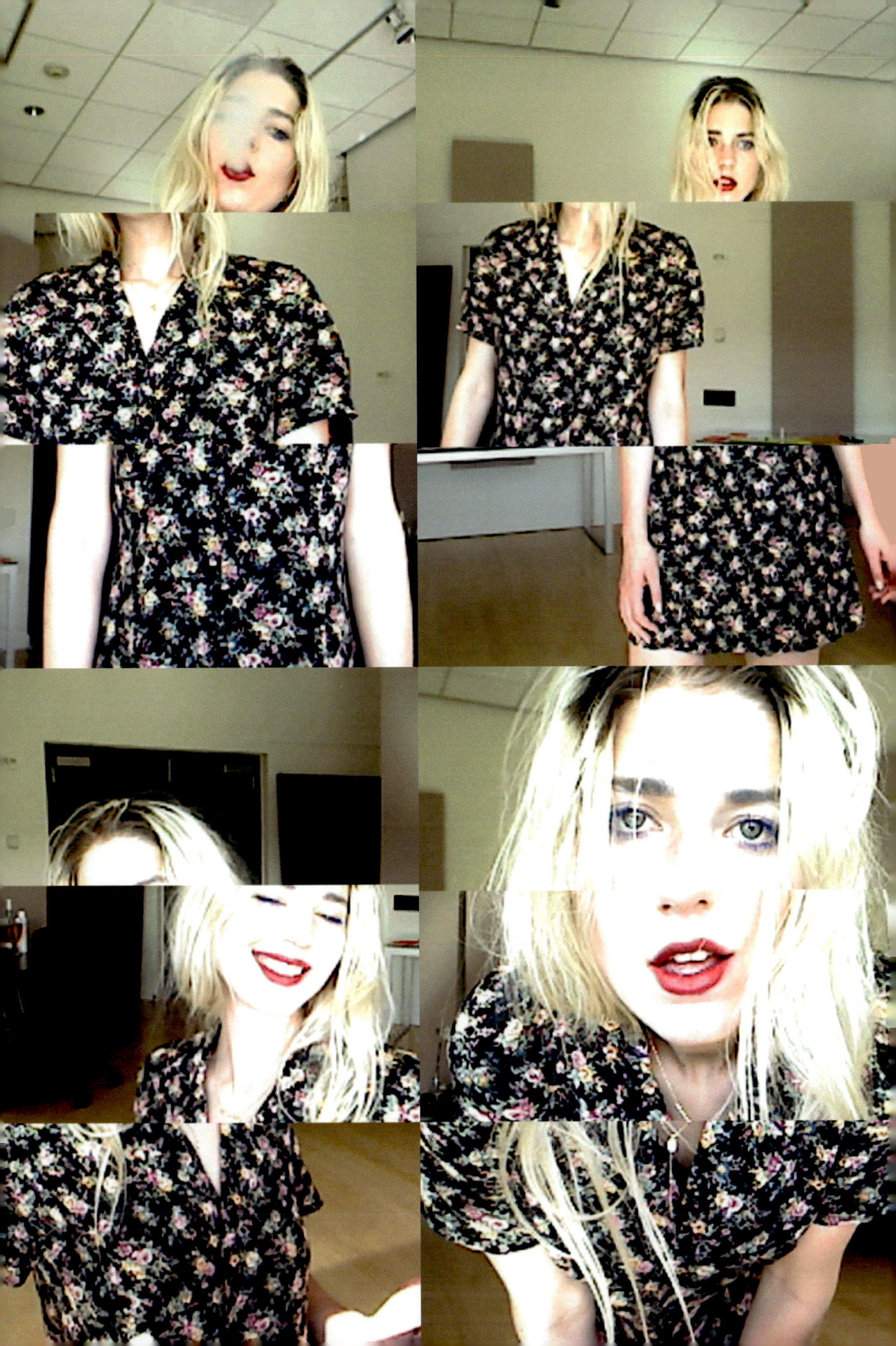

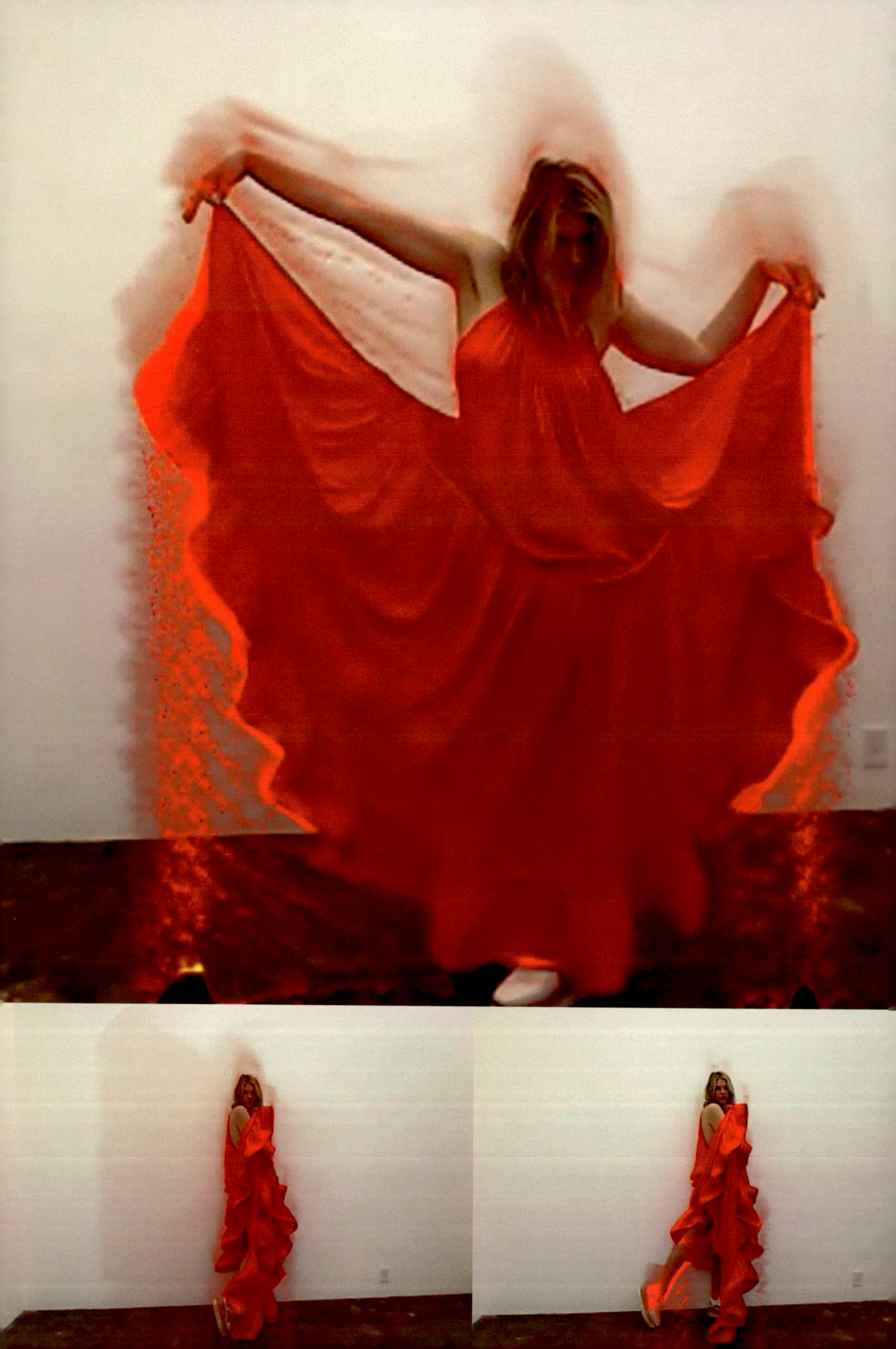

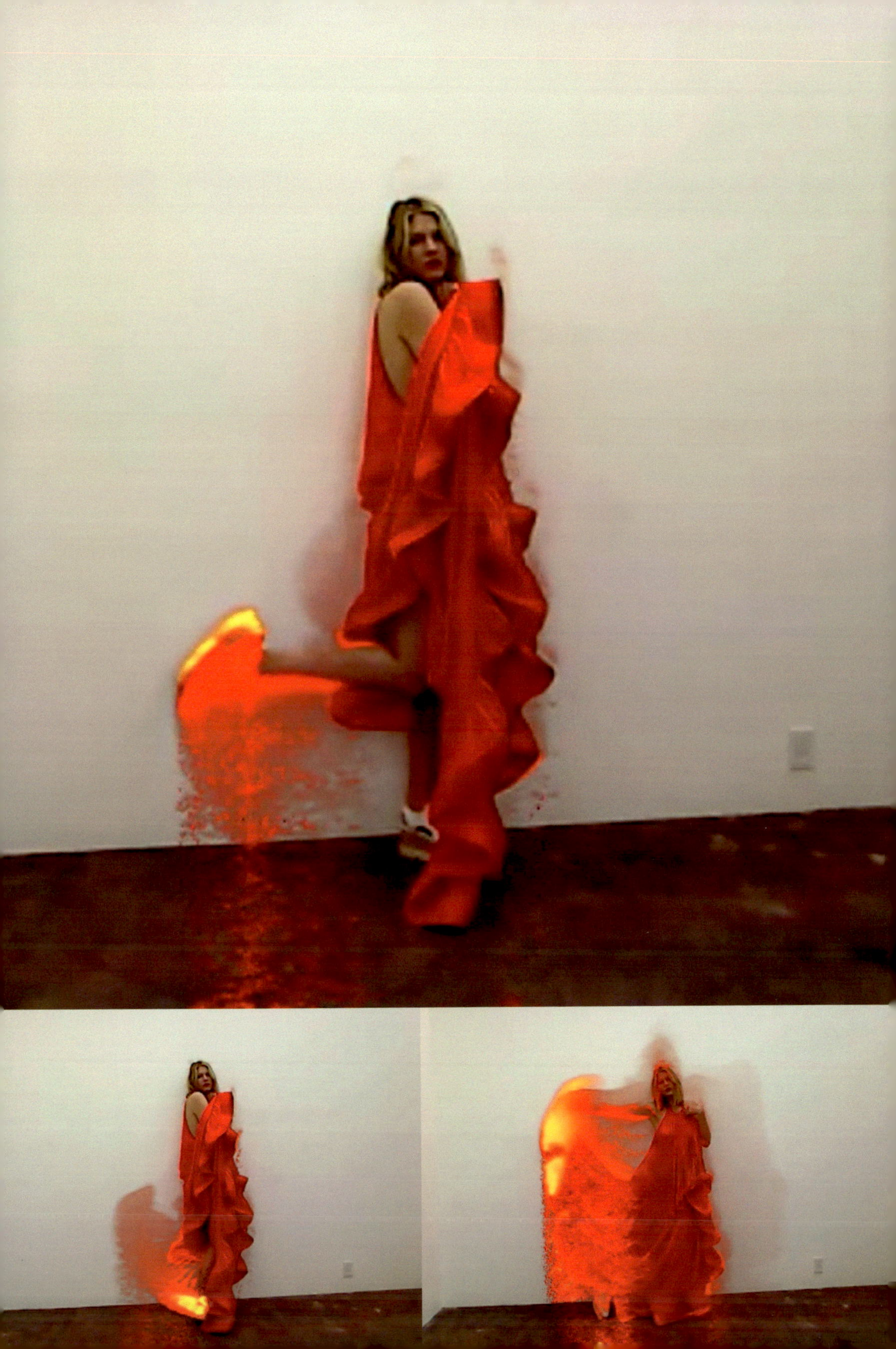

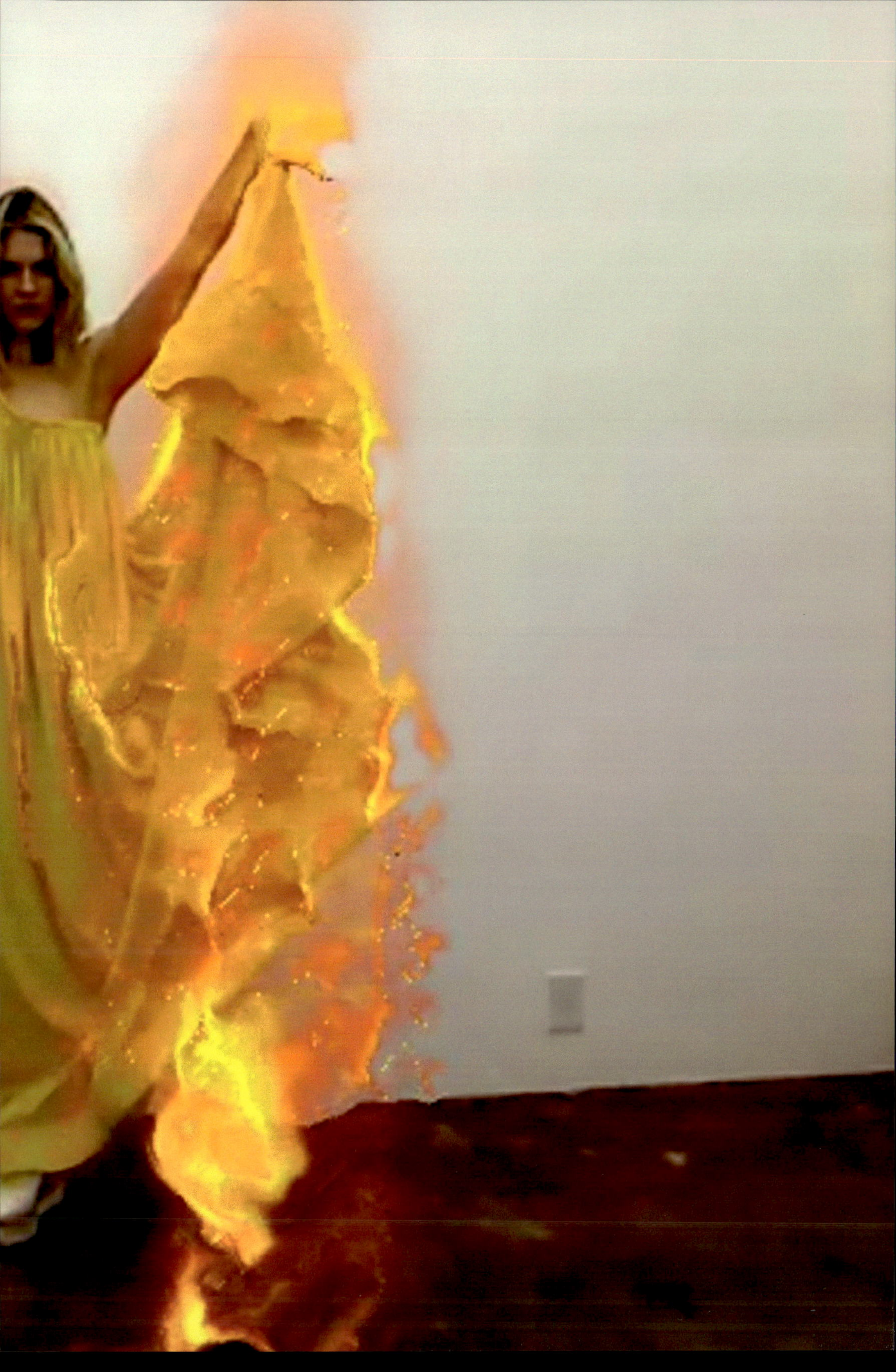

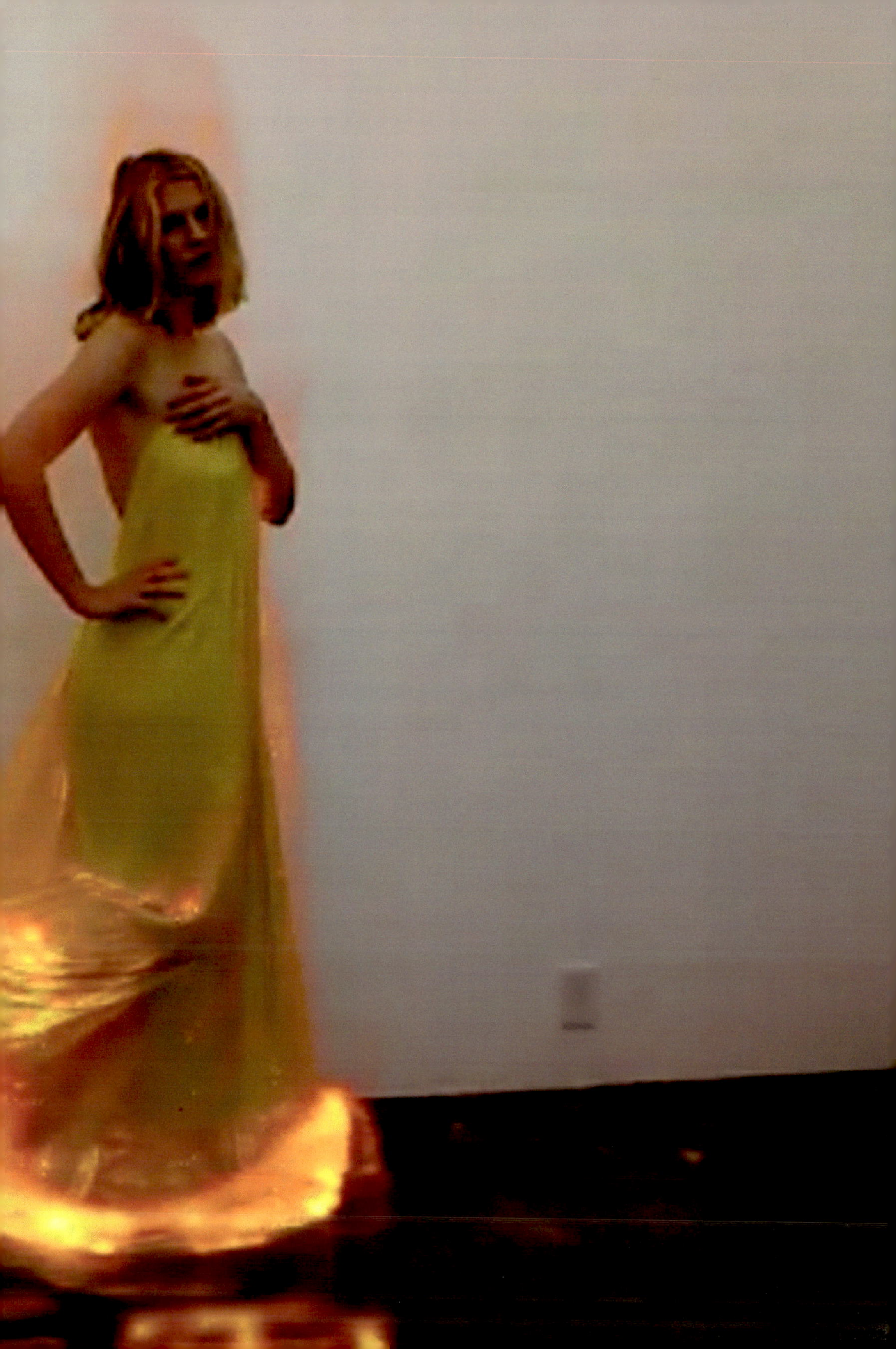

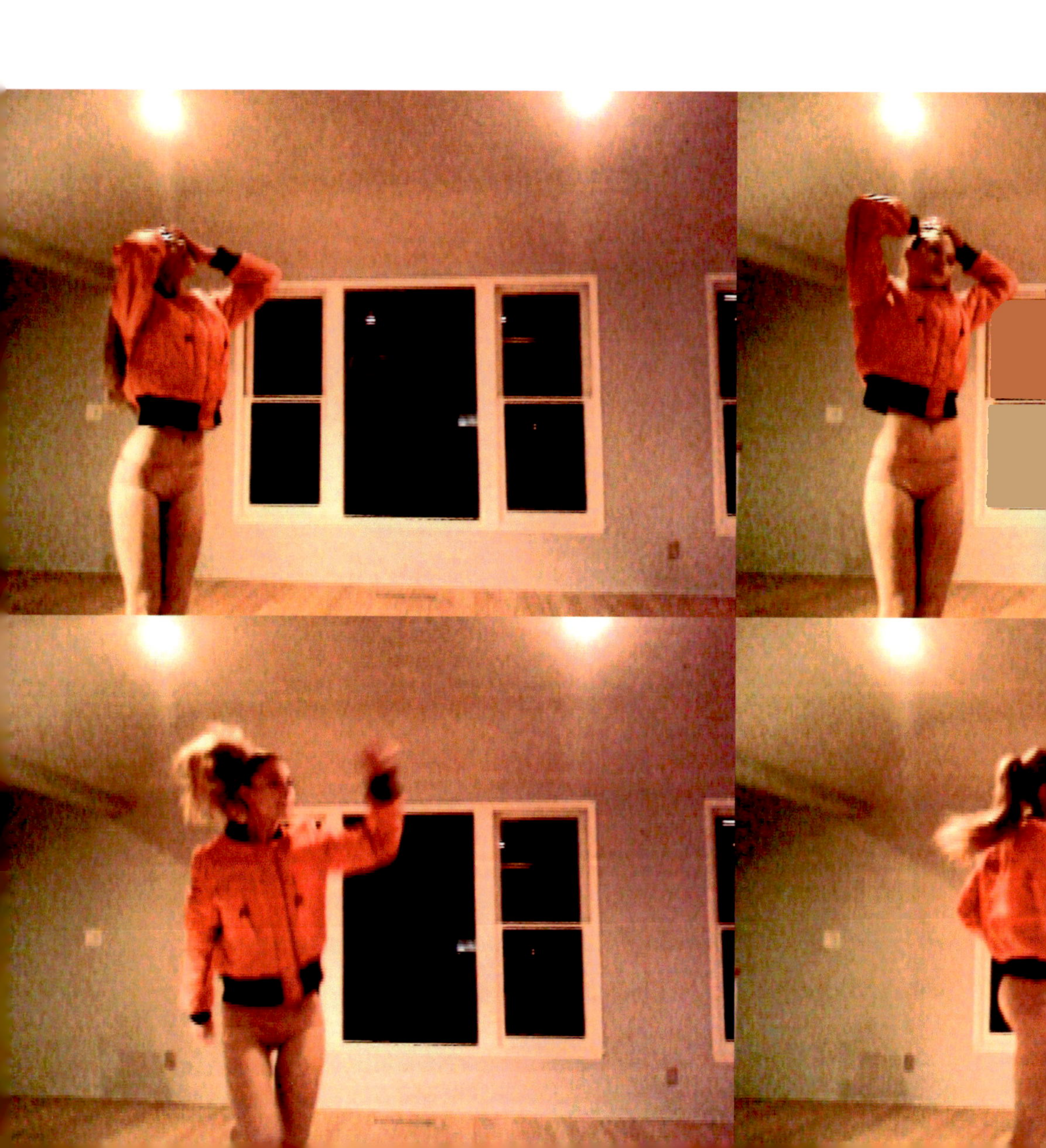

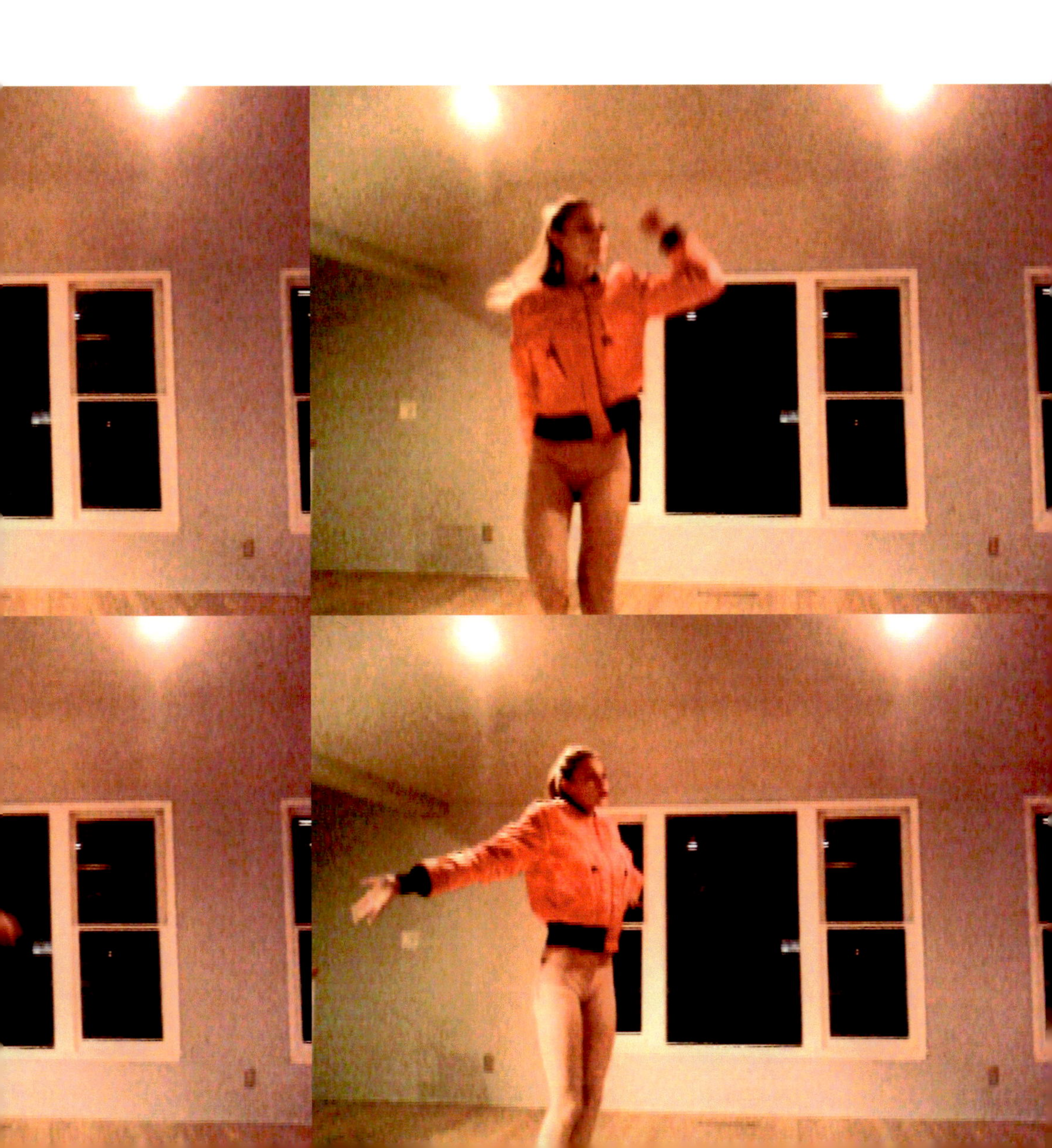

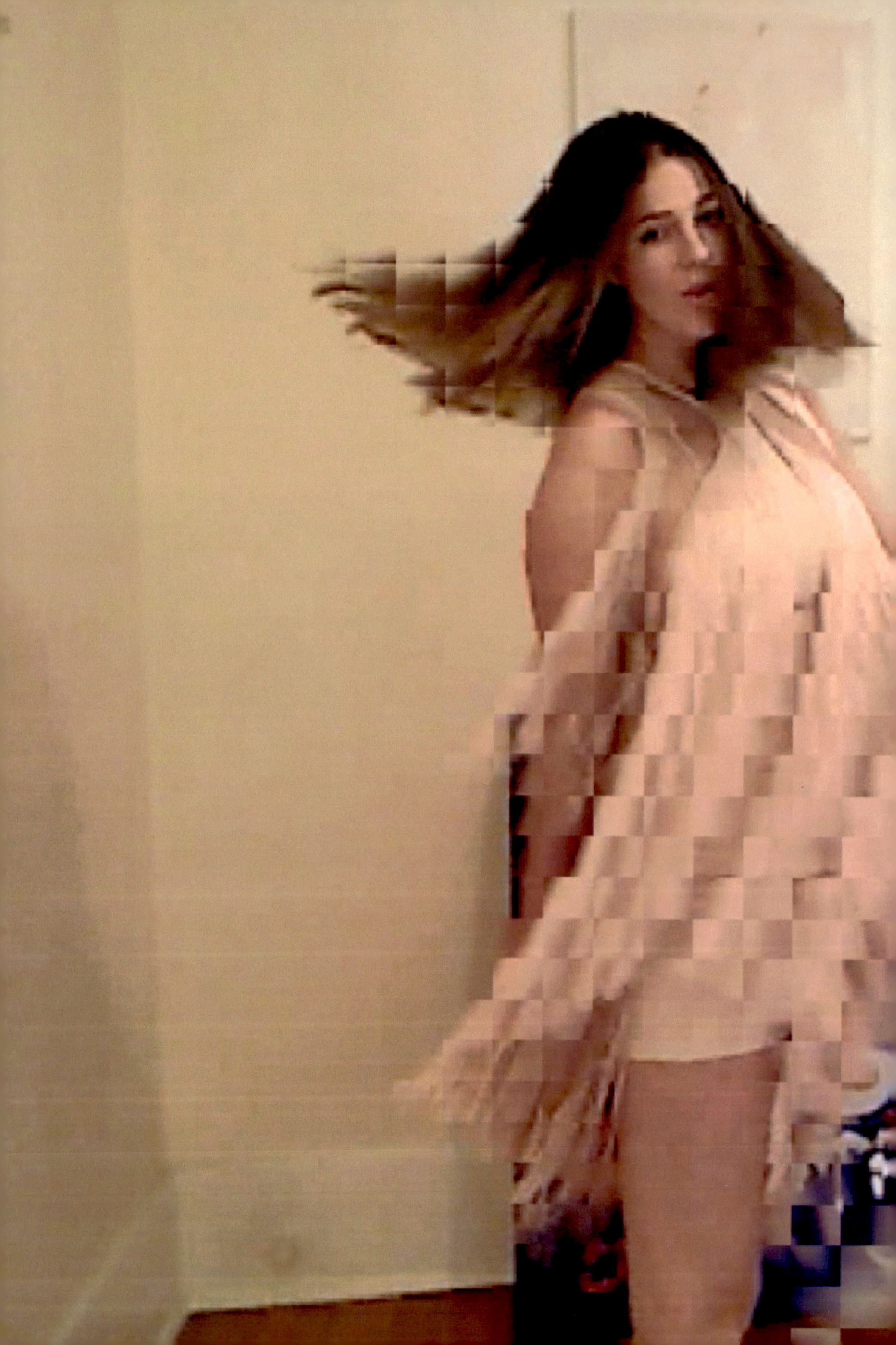

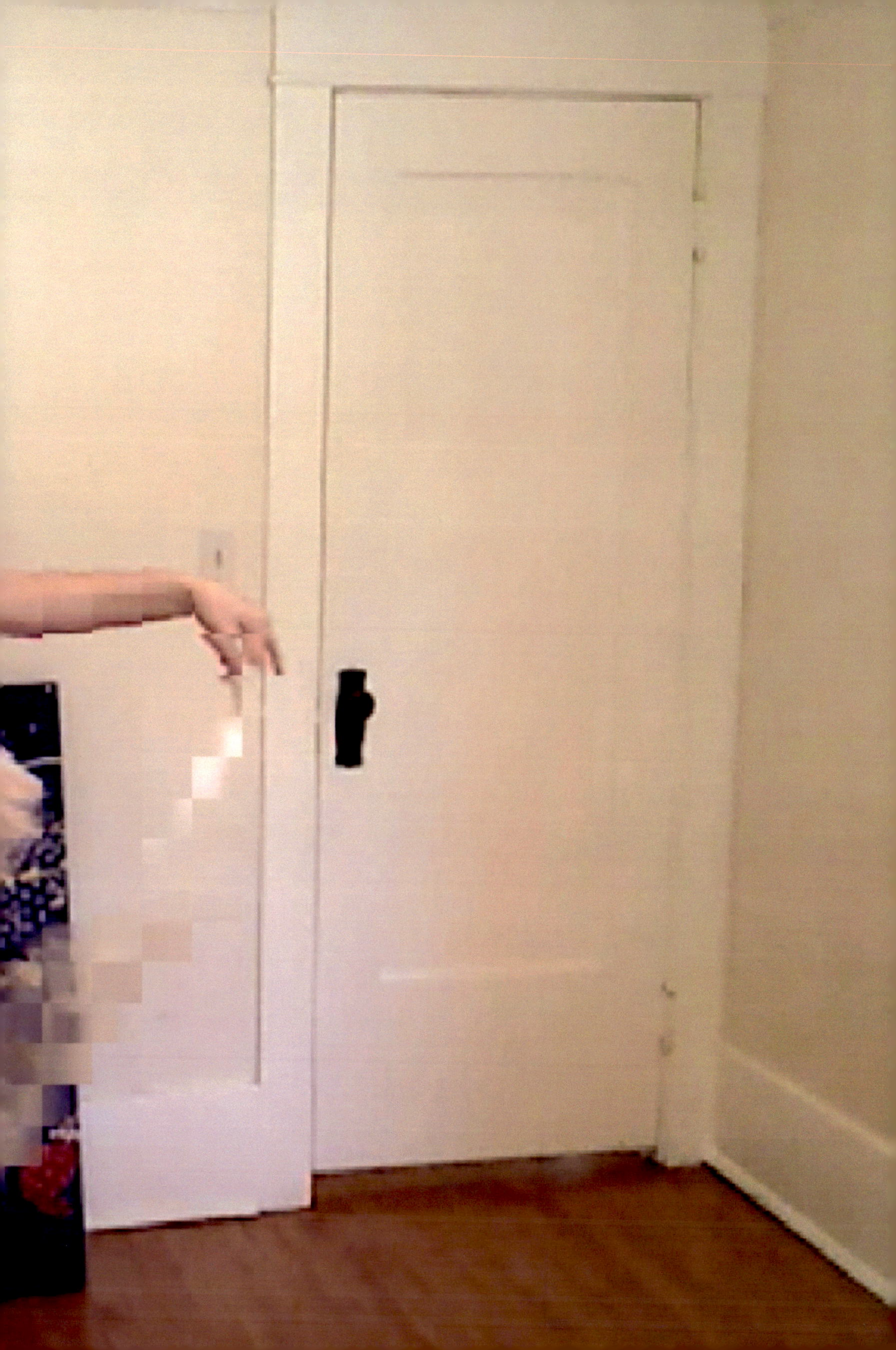

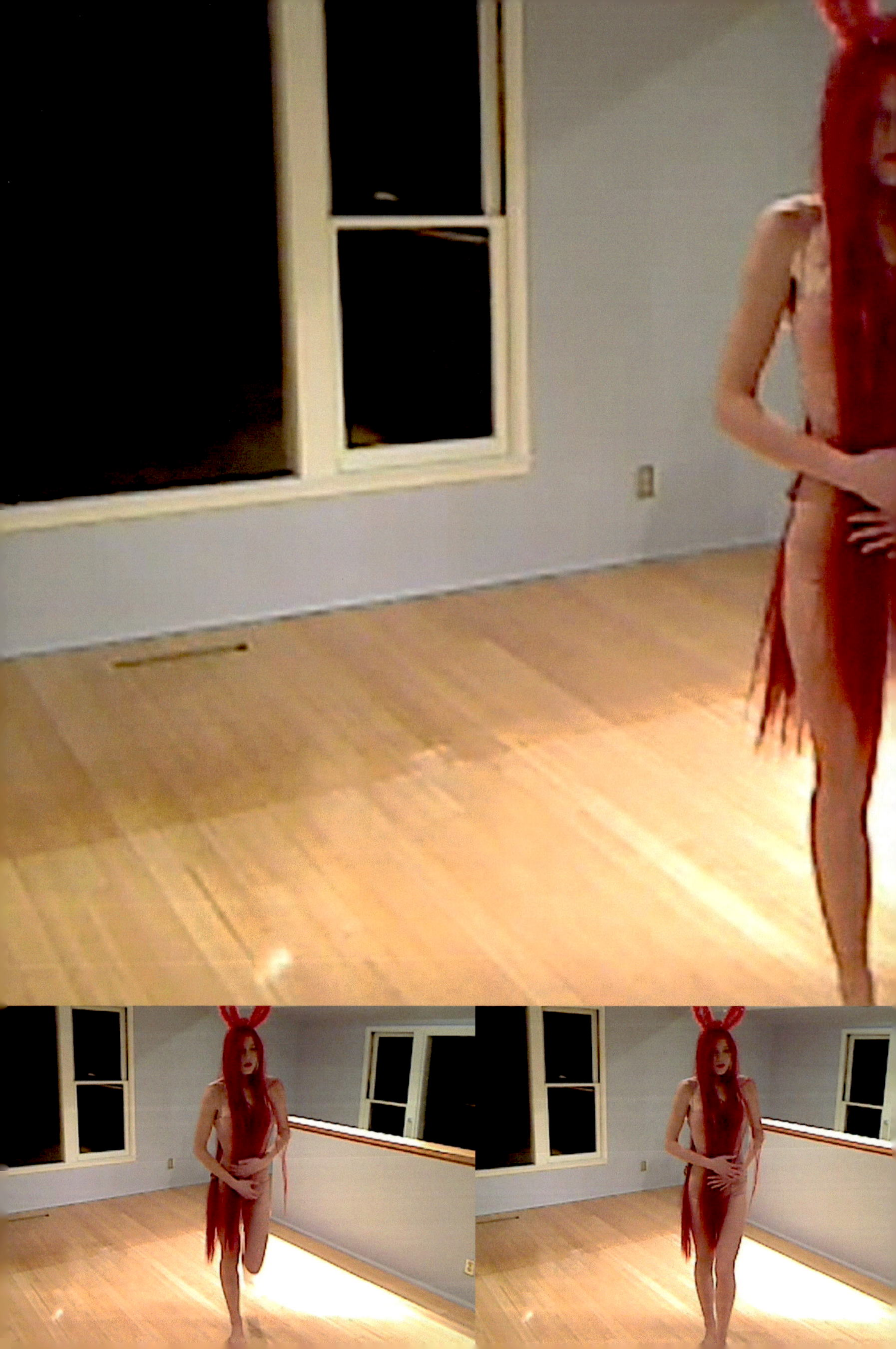

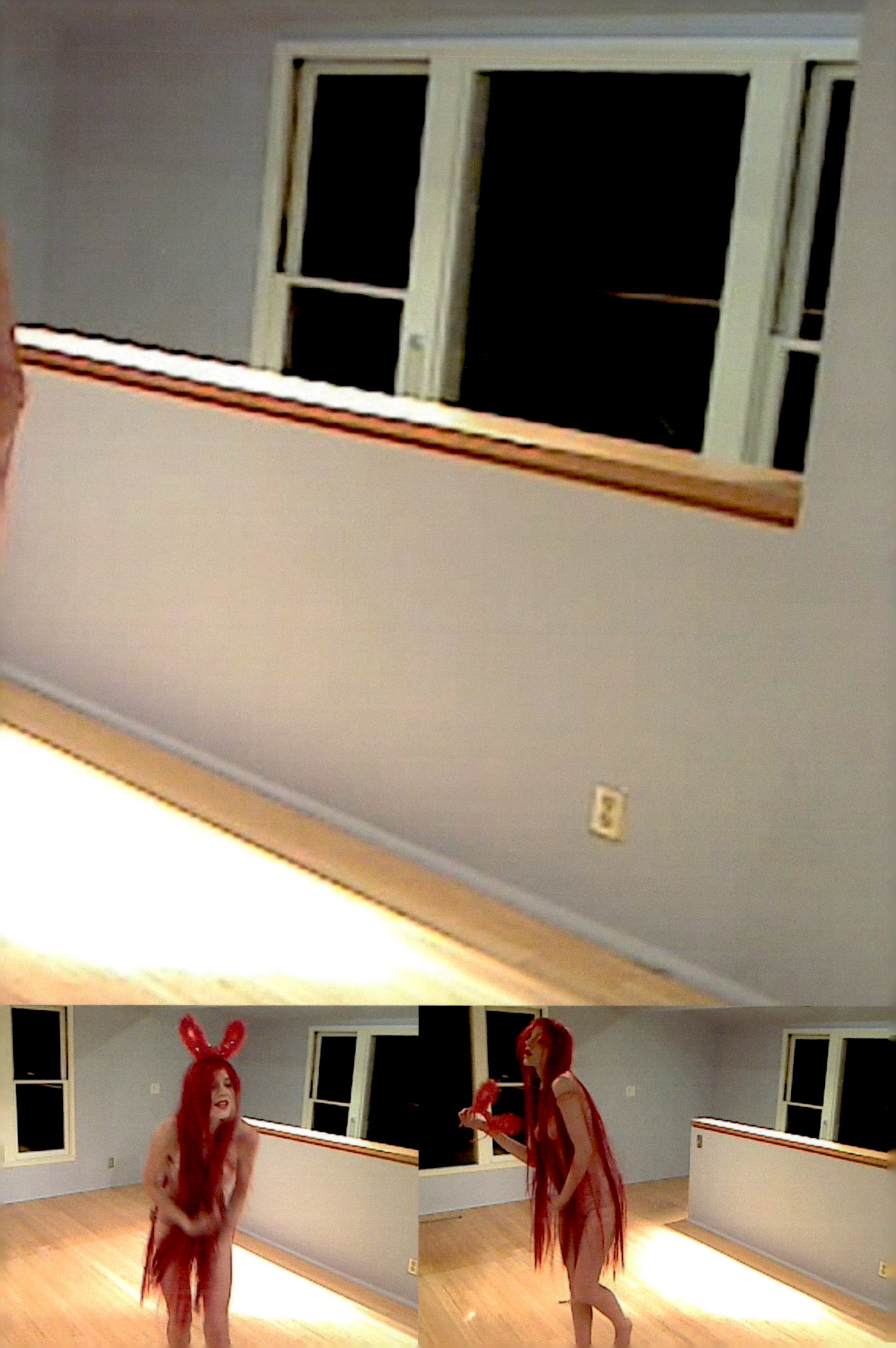

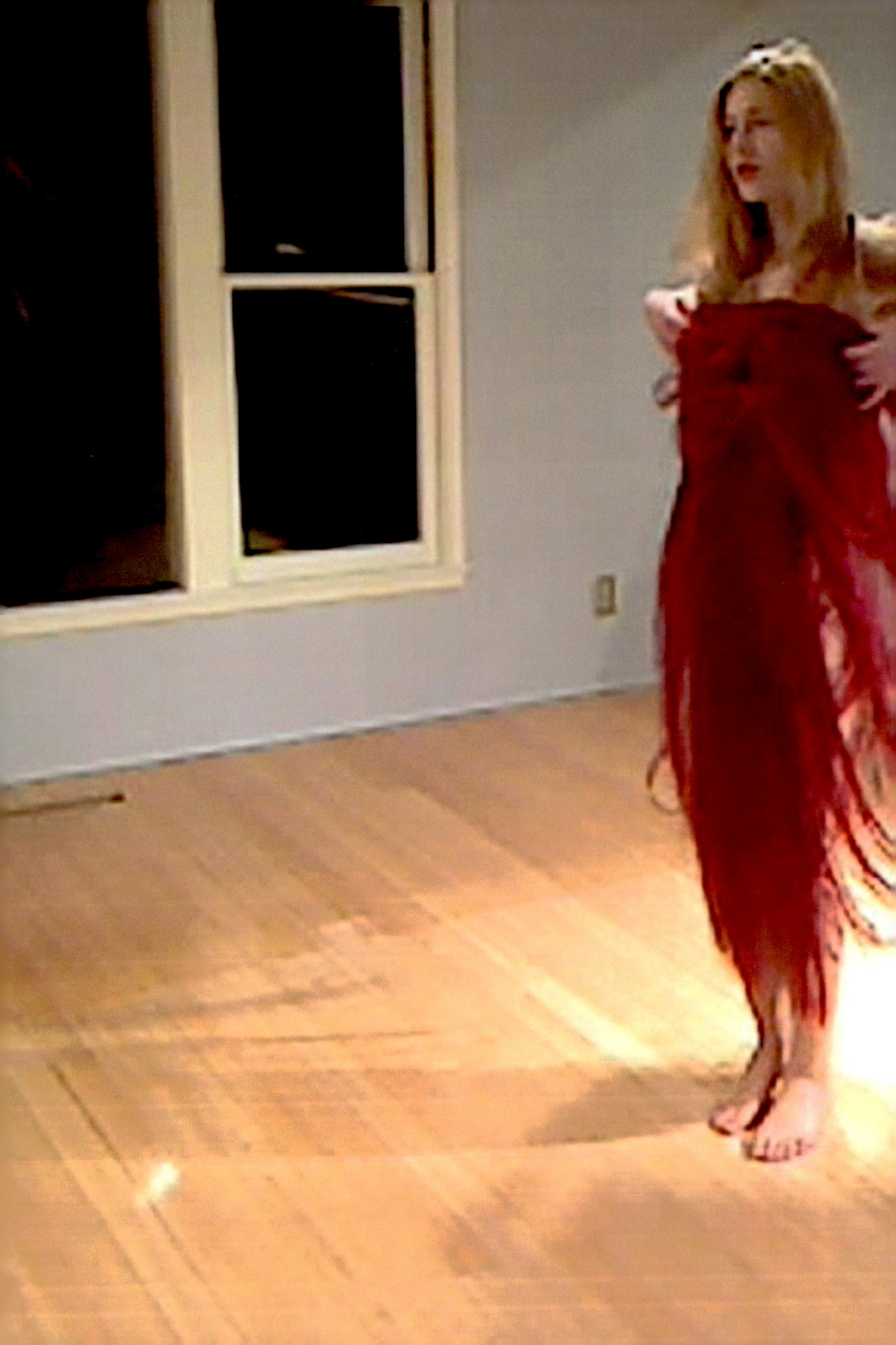

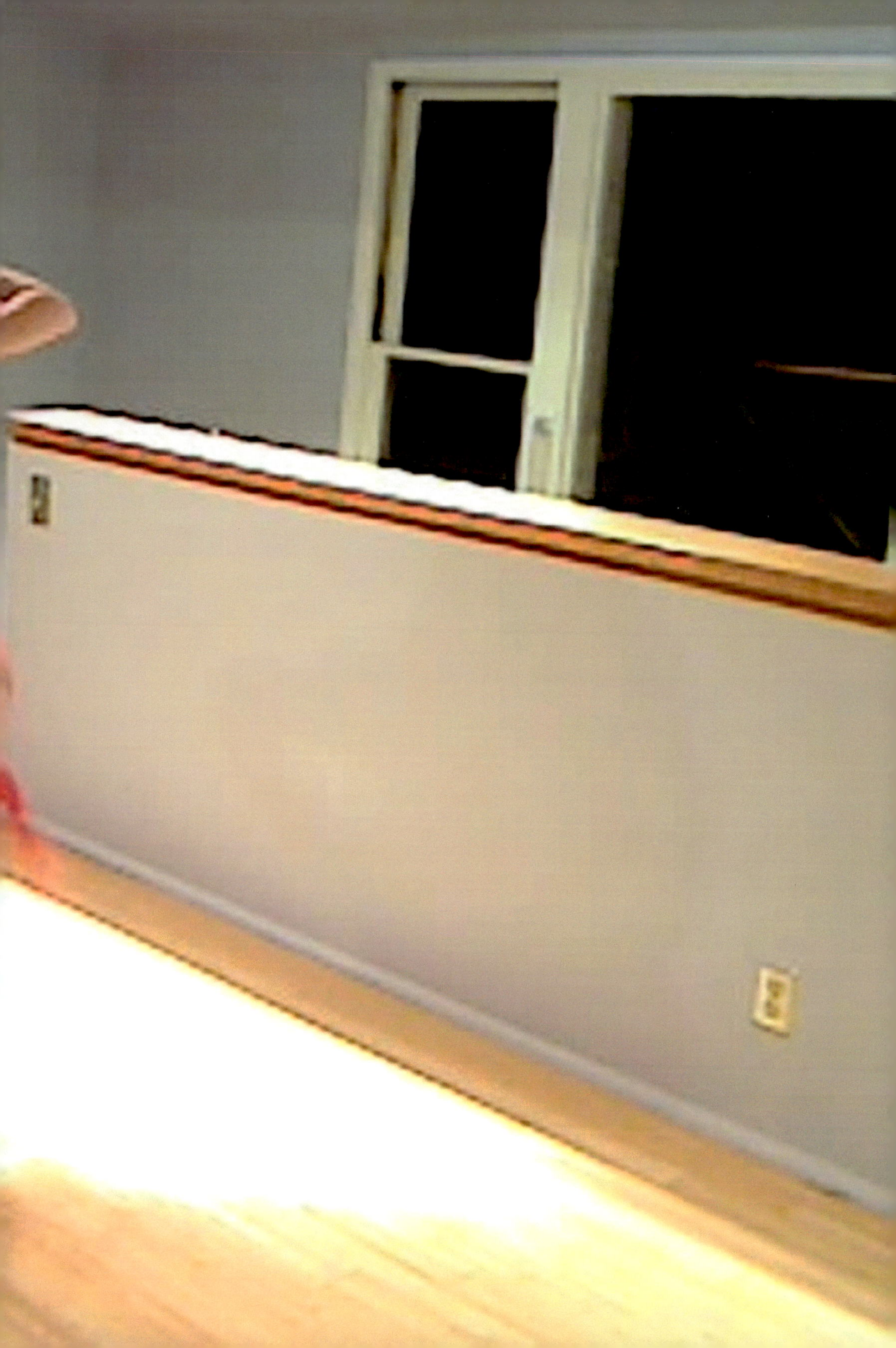

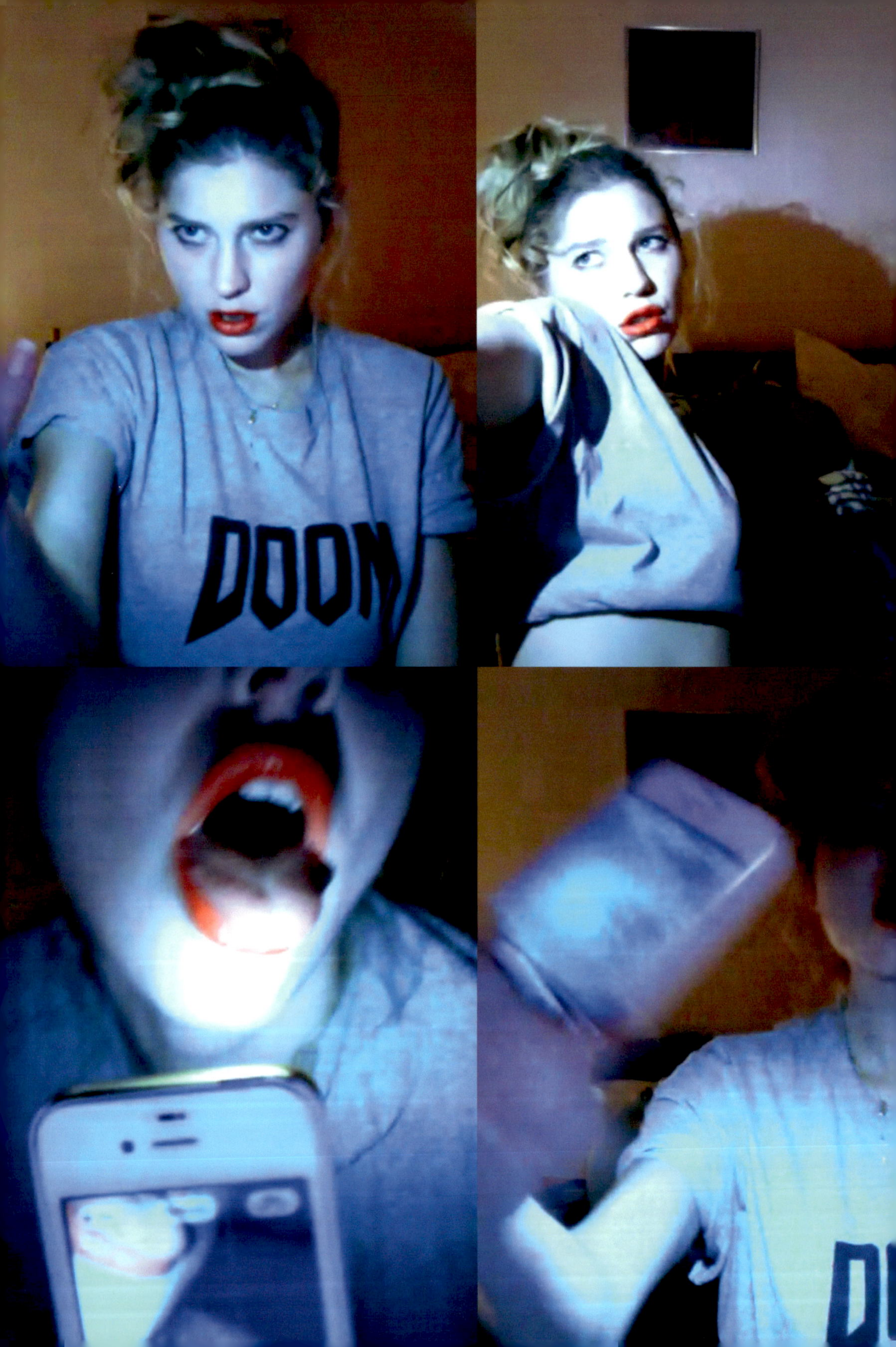
DOOM

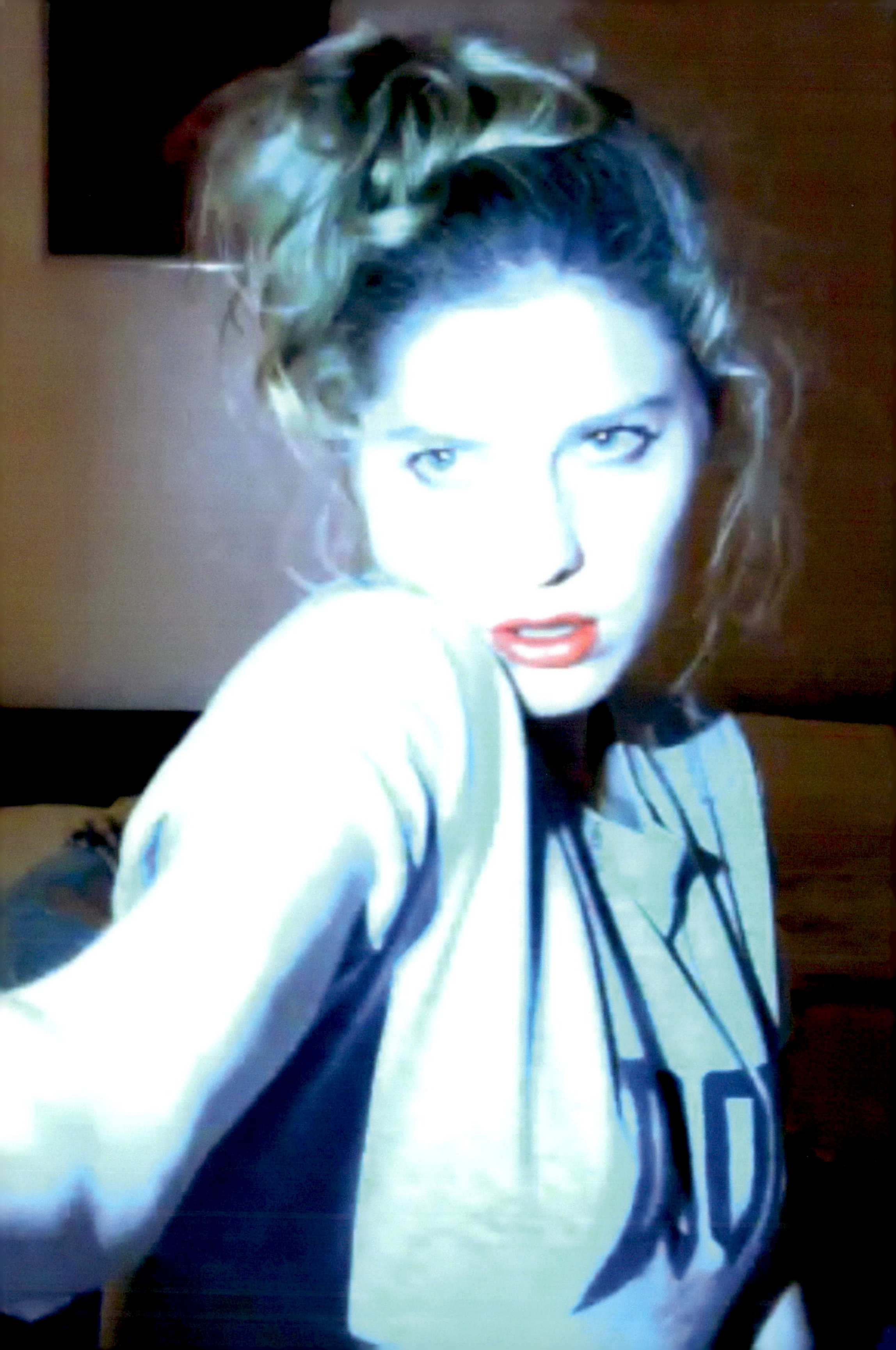

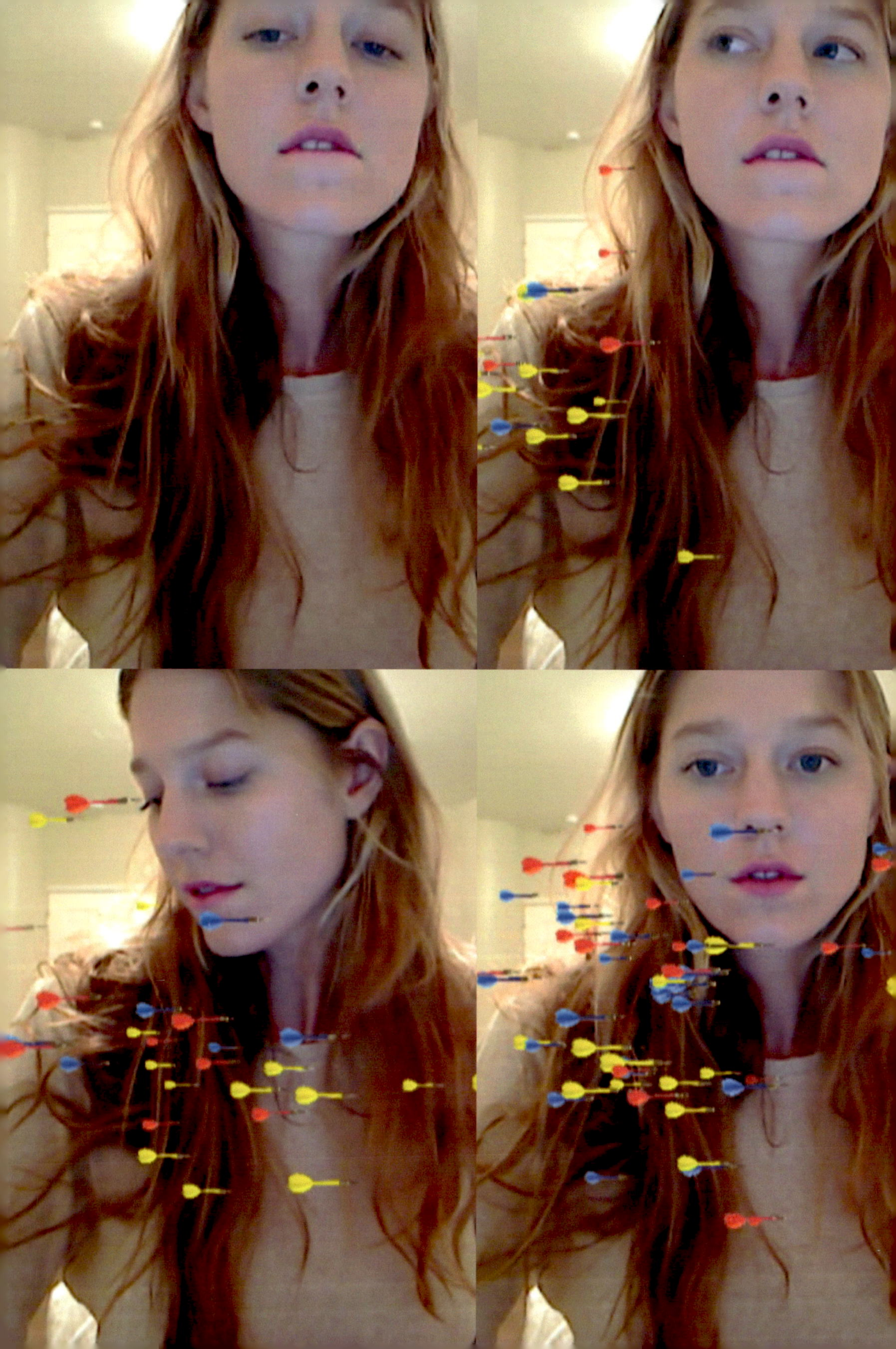

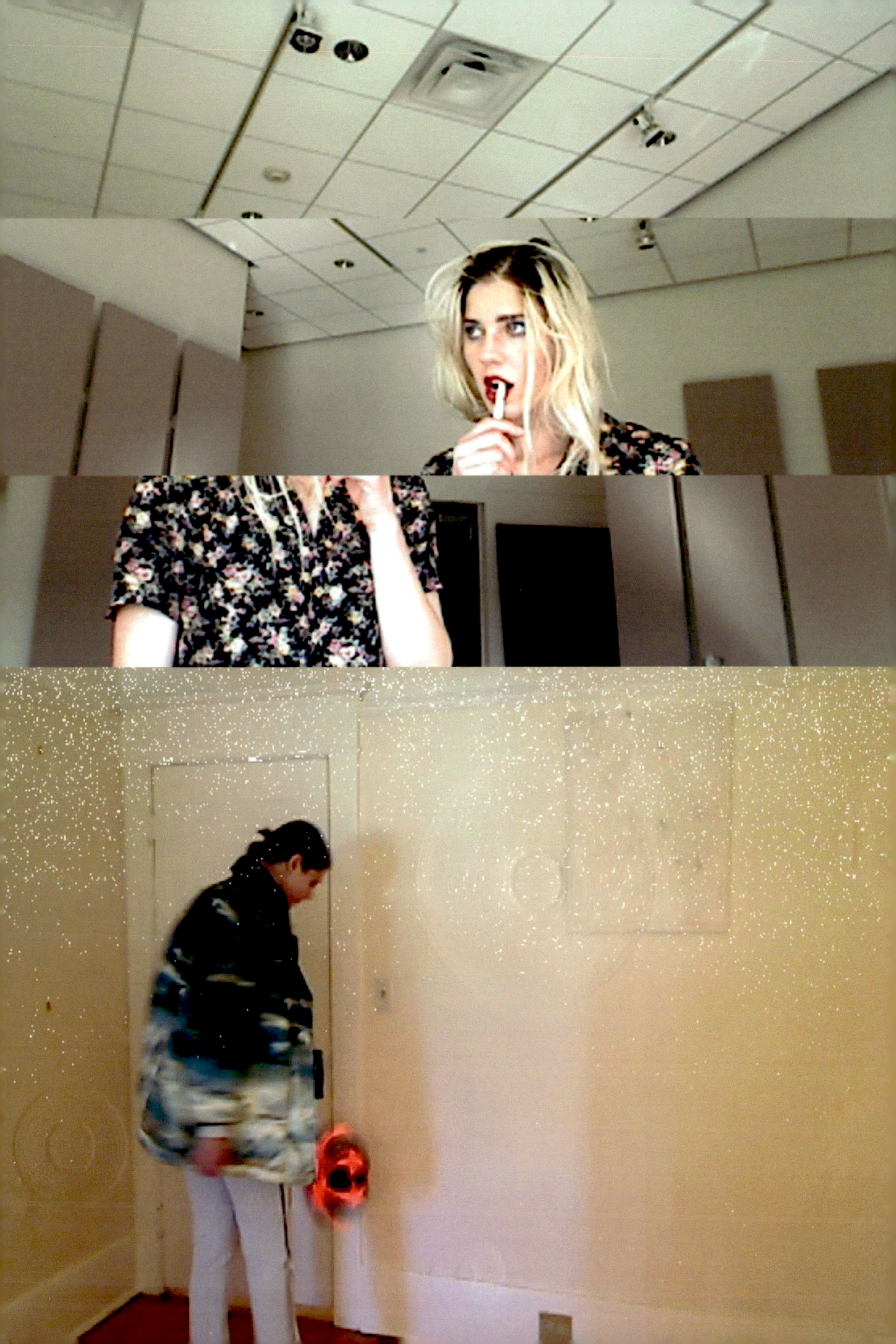

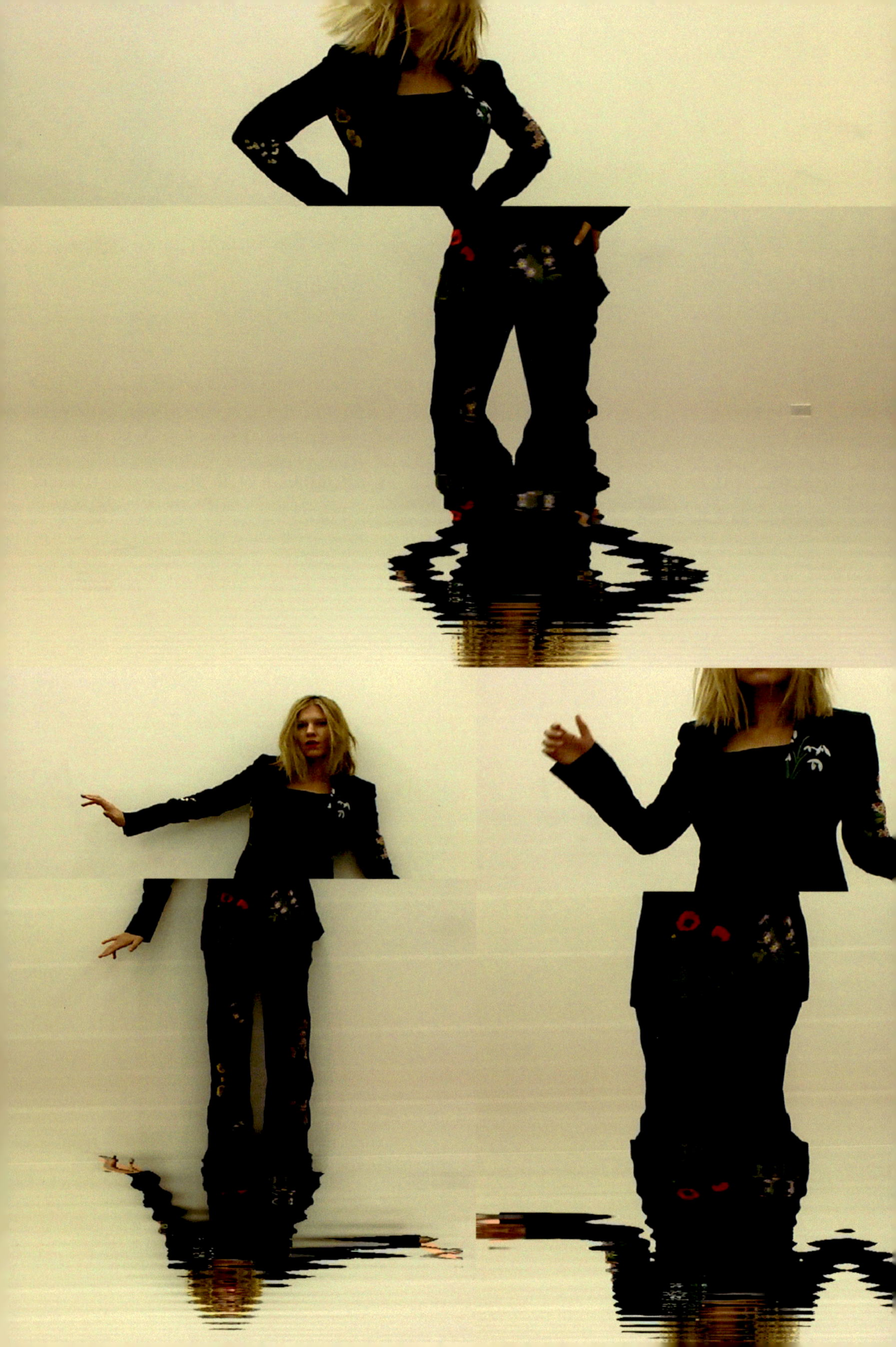

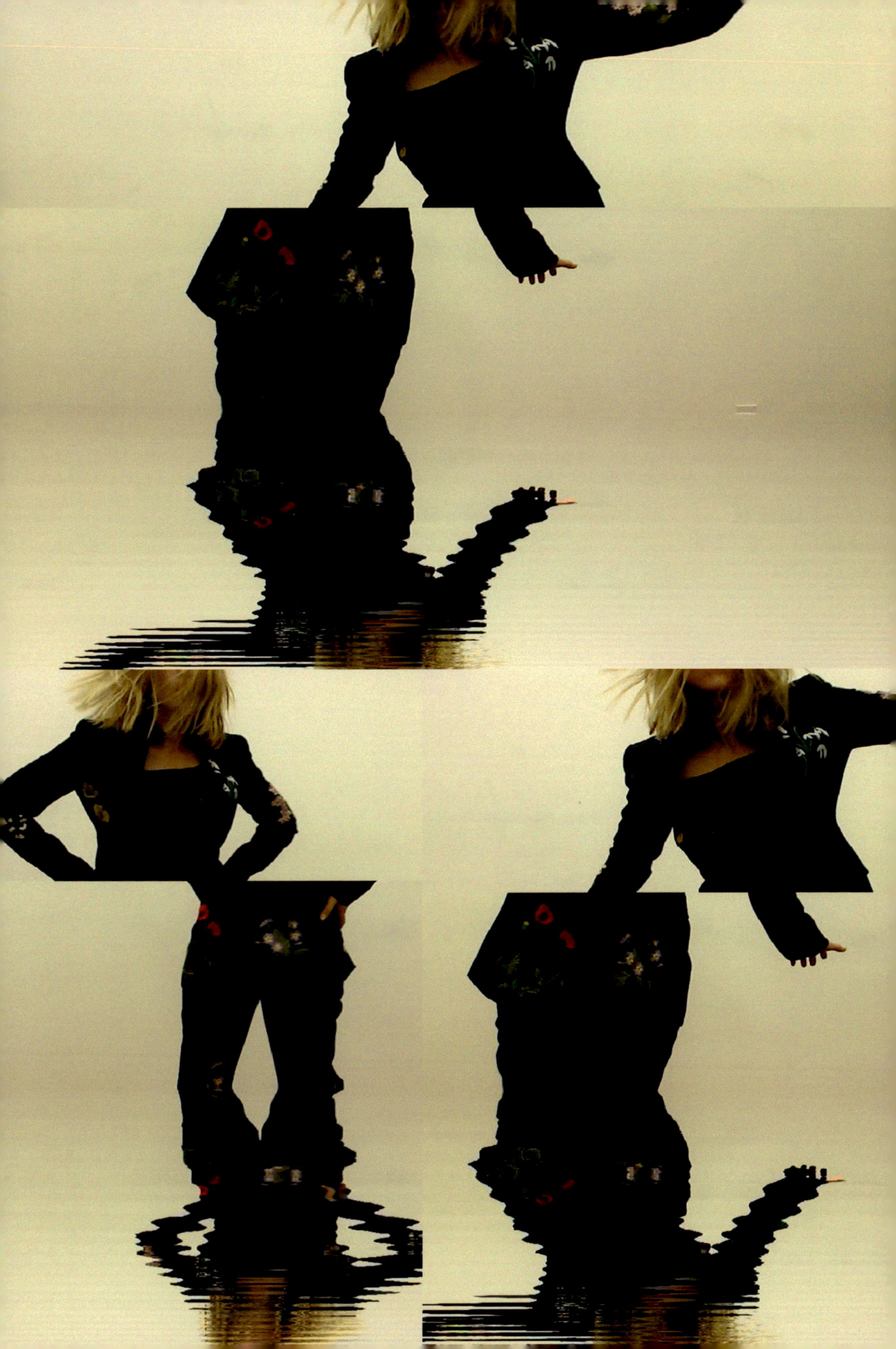

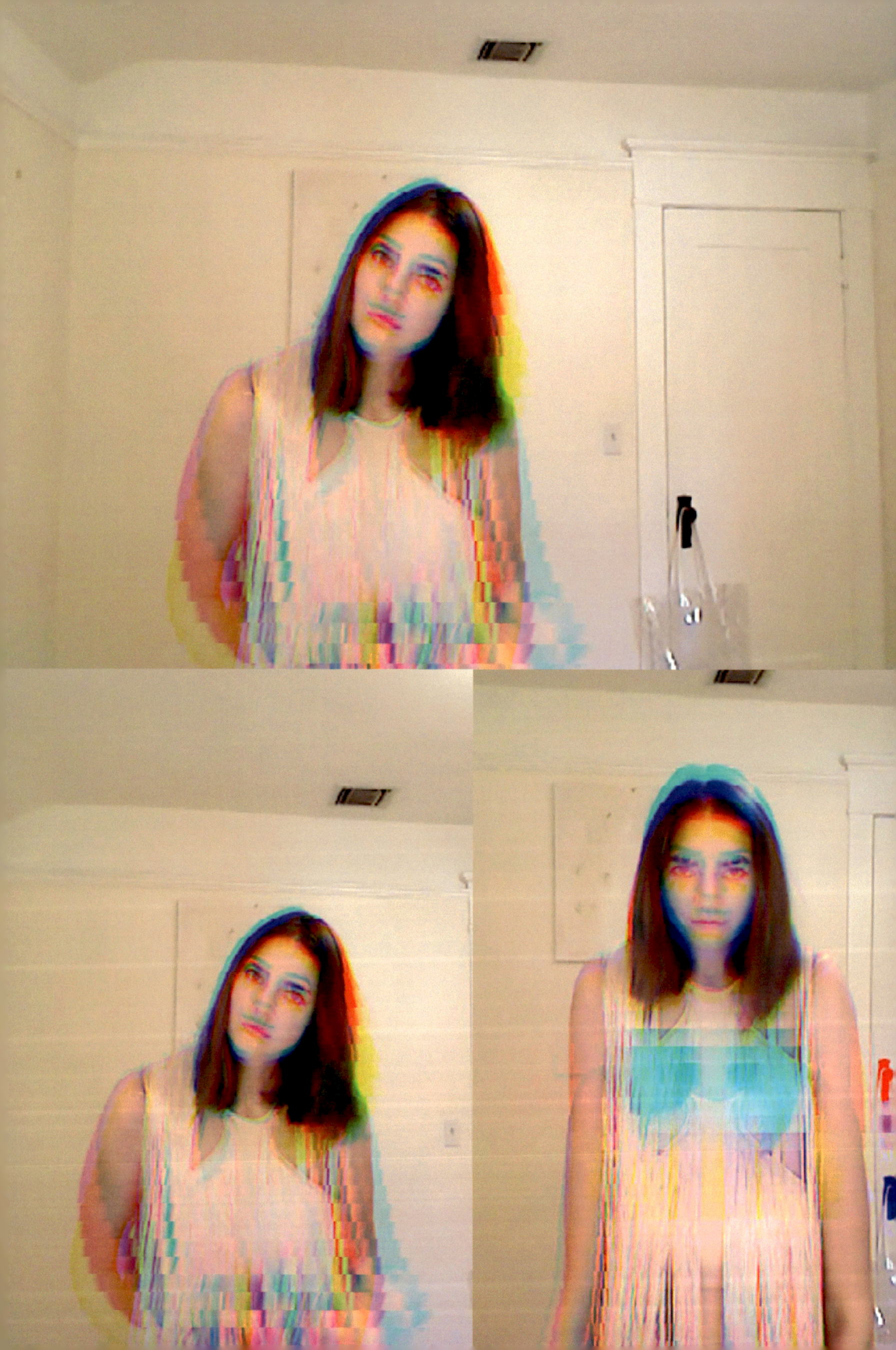

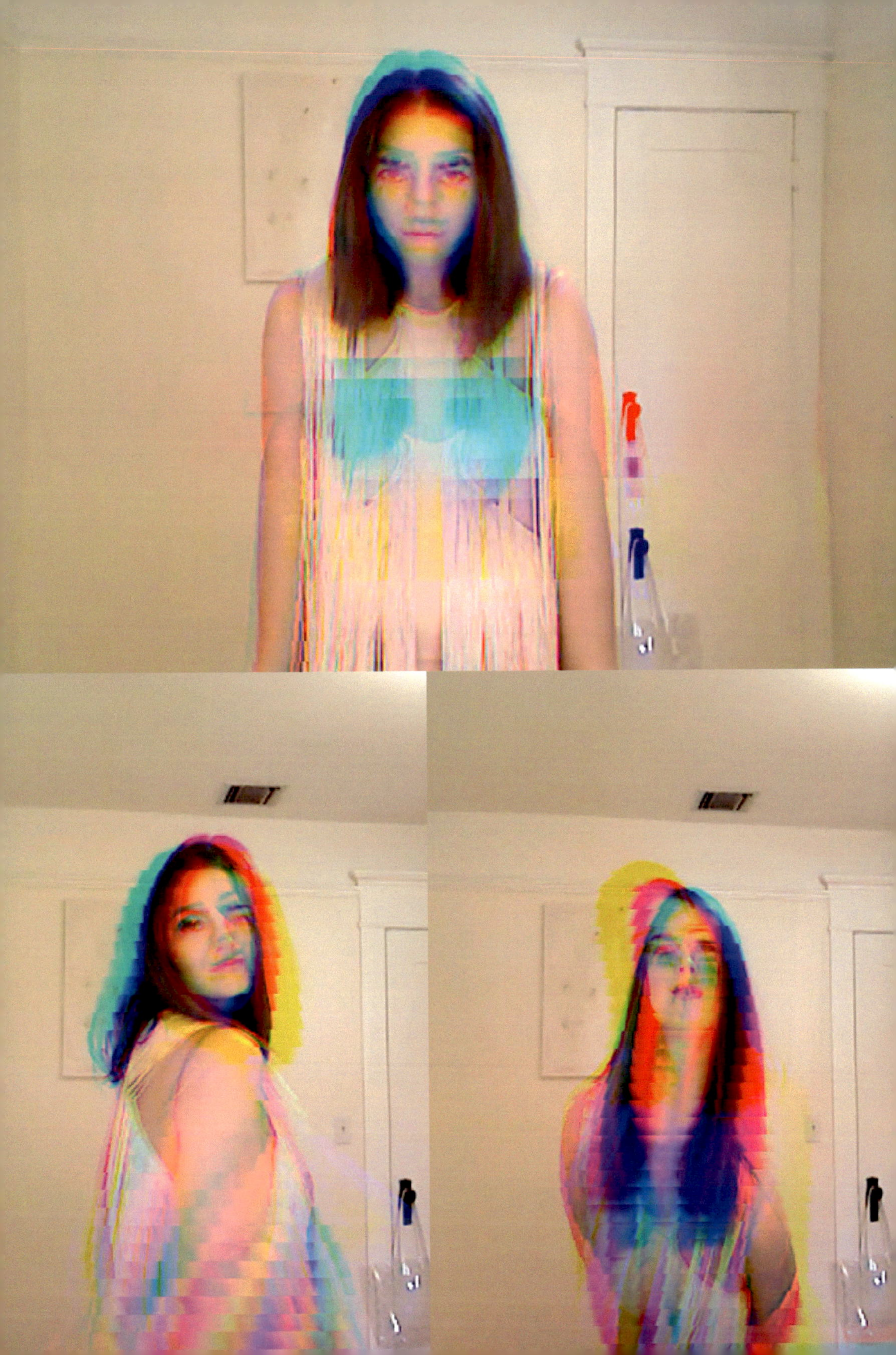

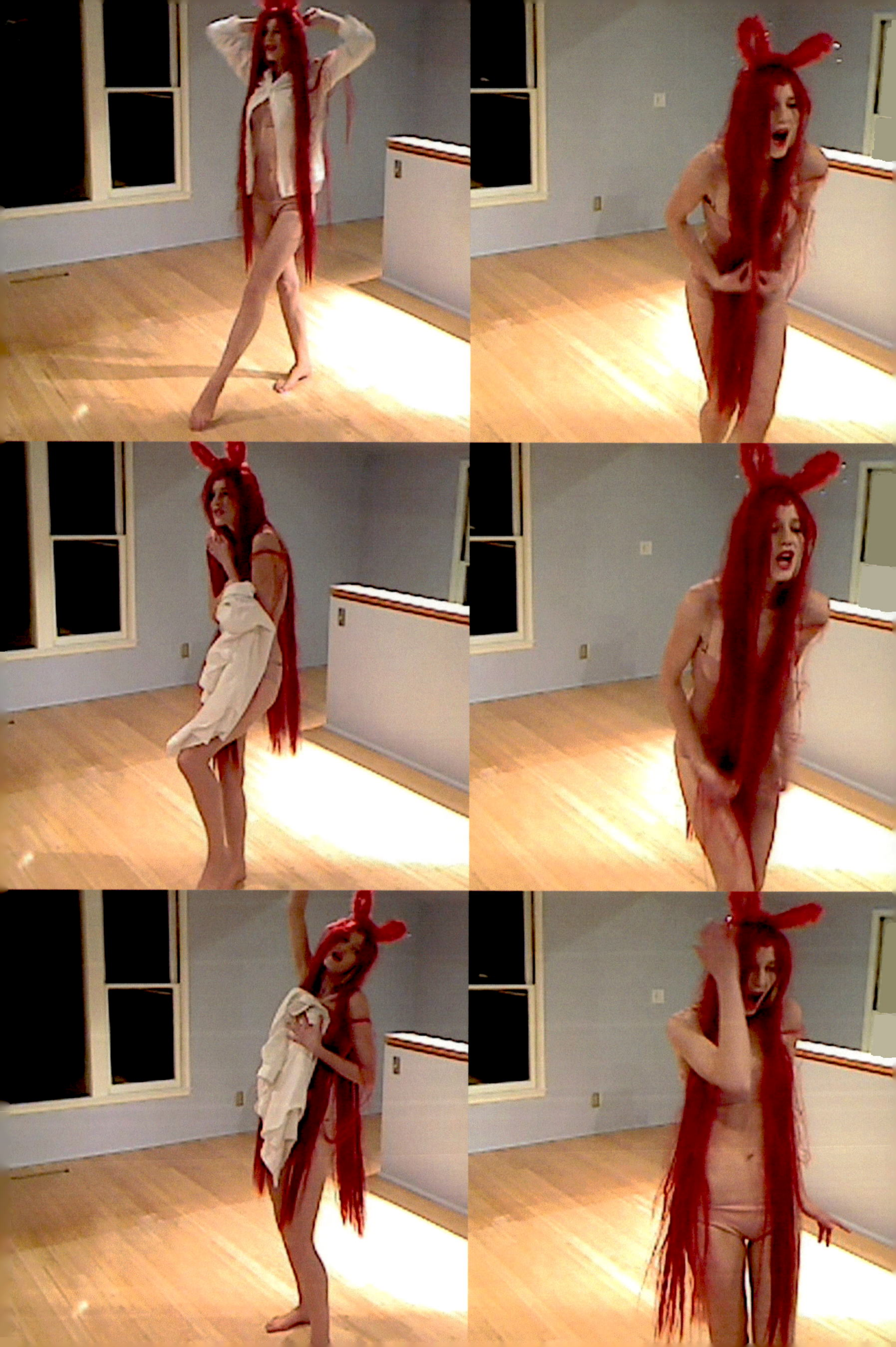

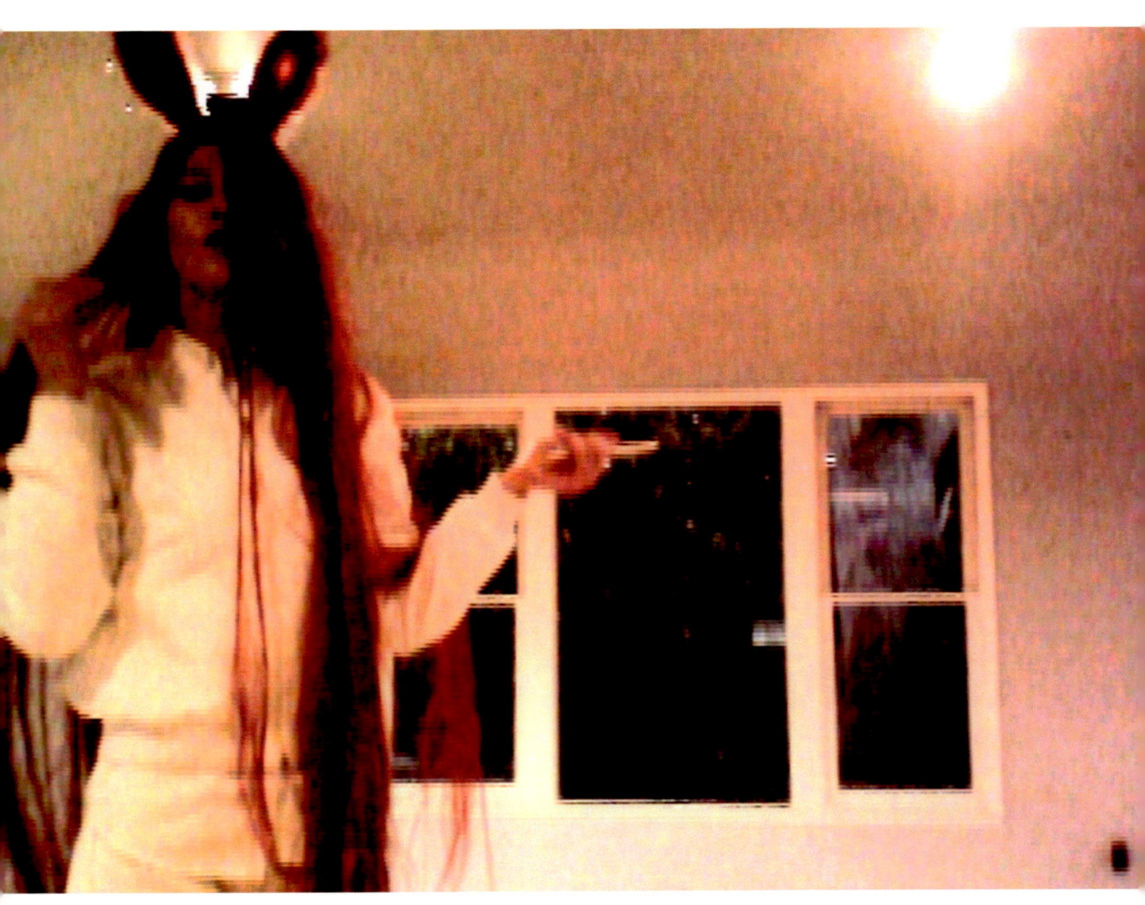

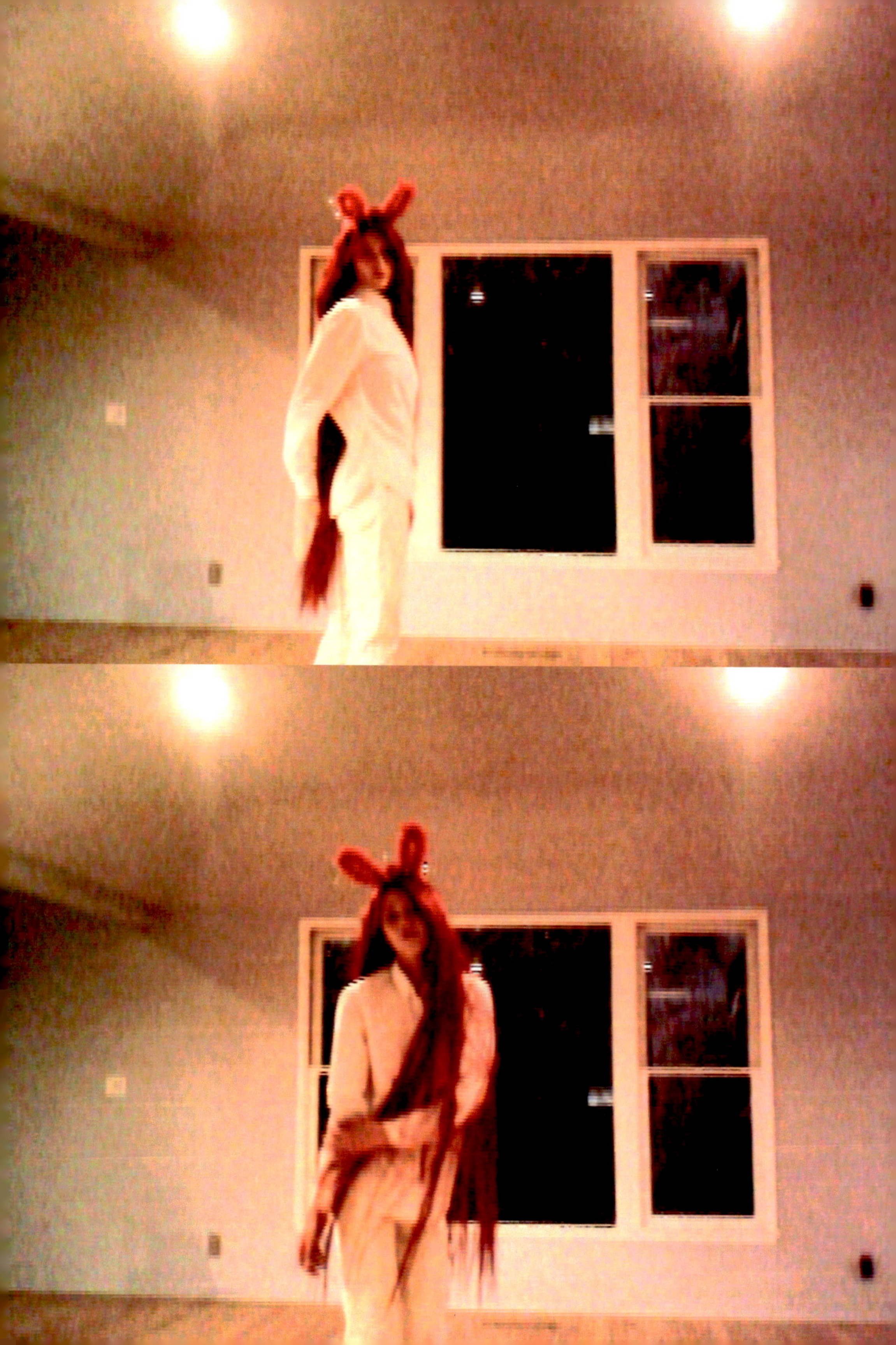

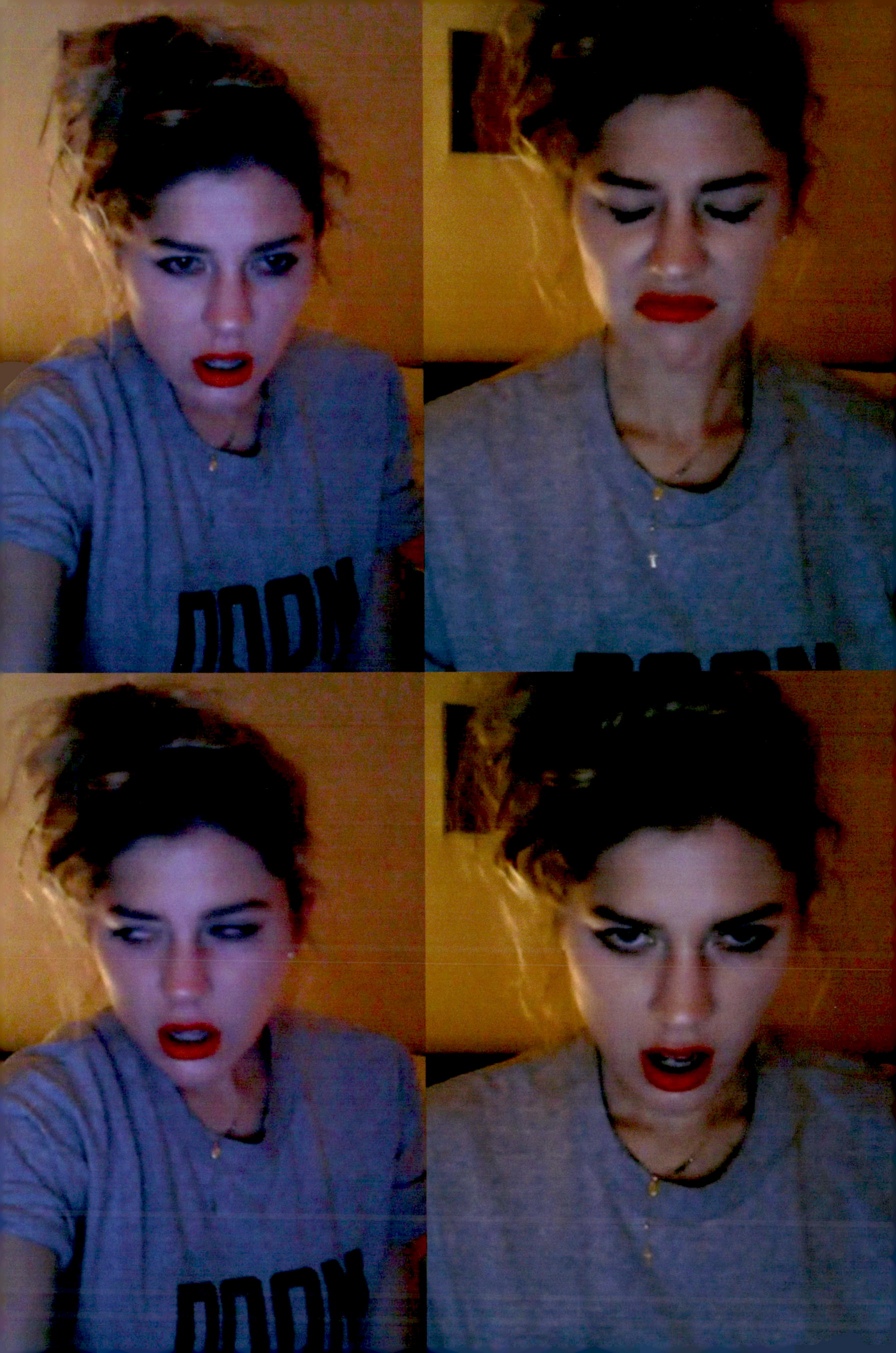

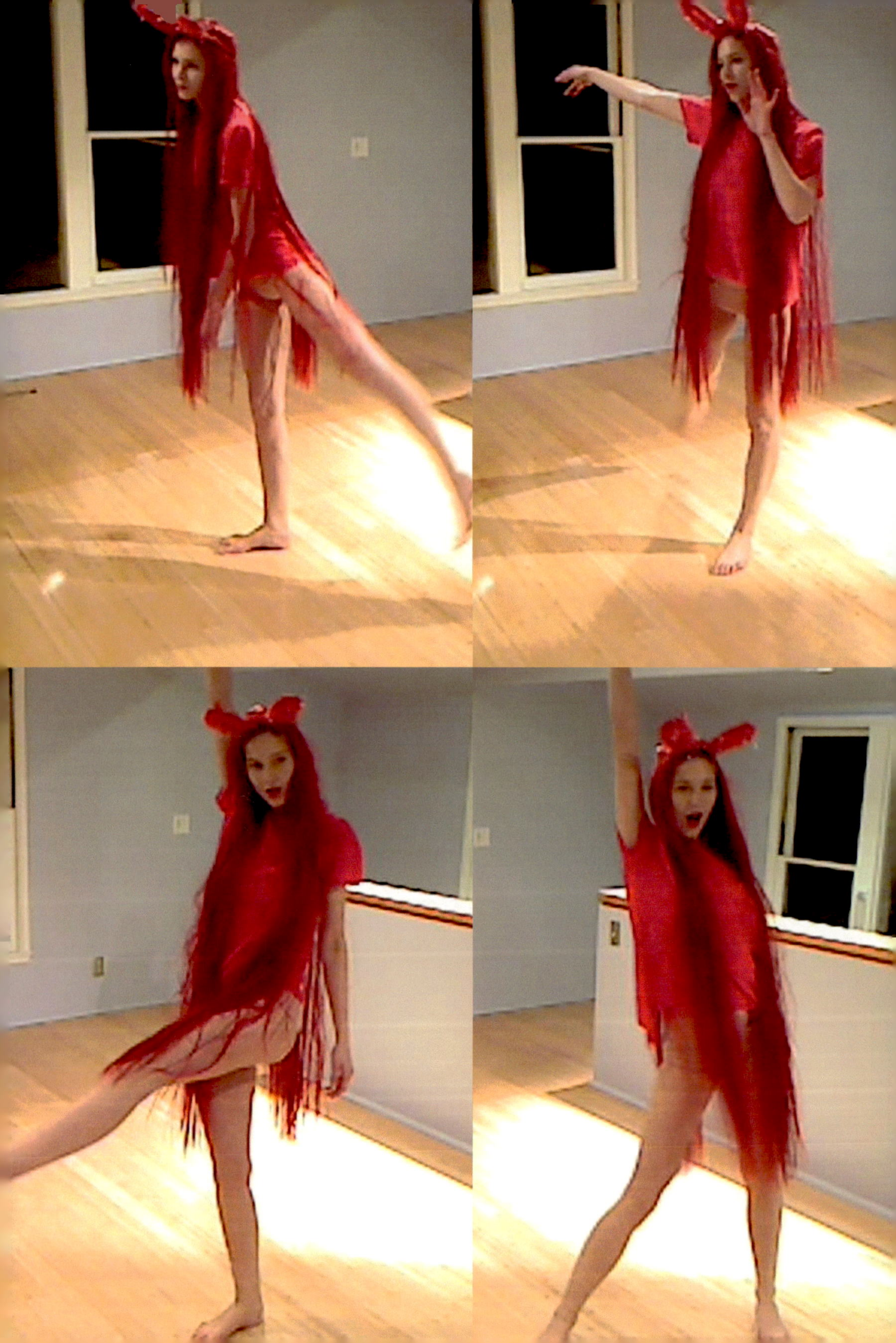

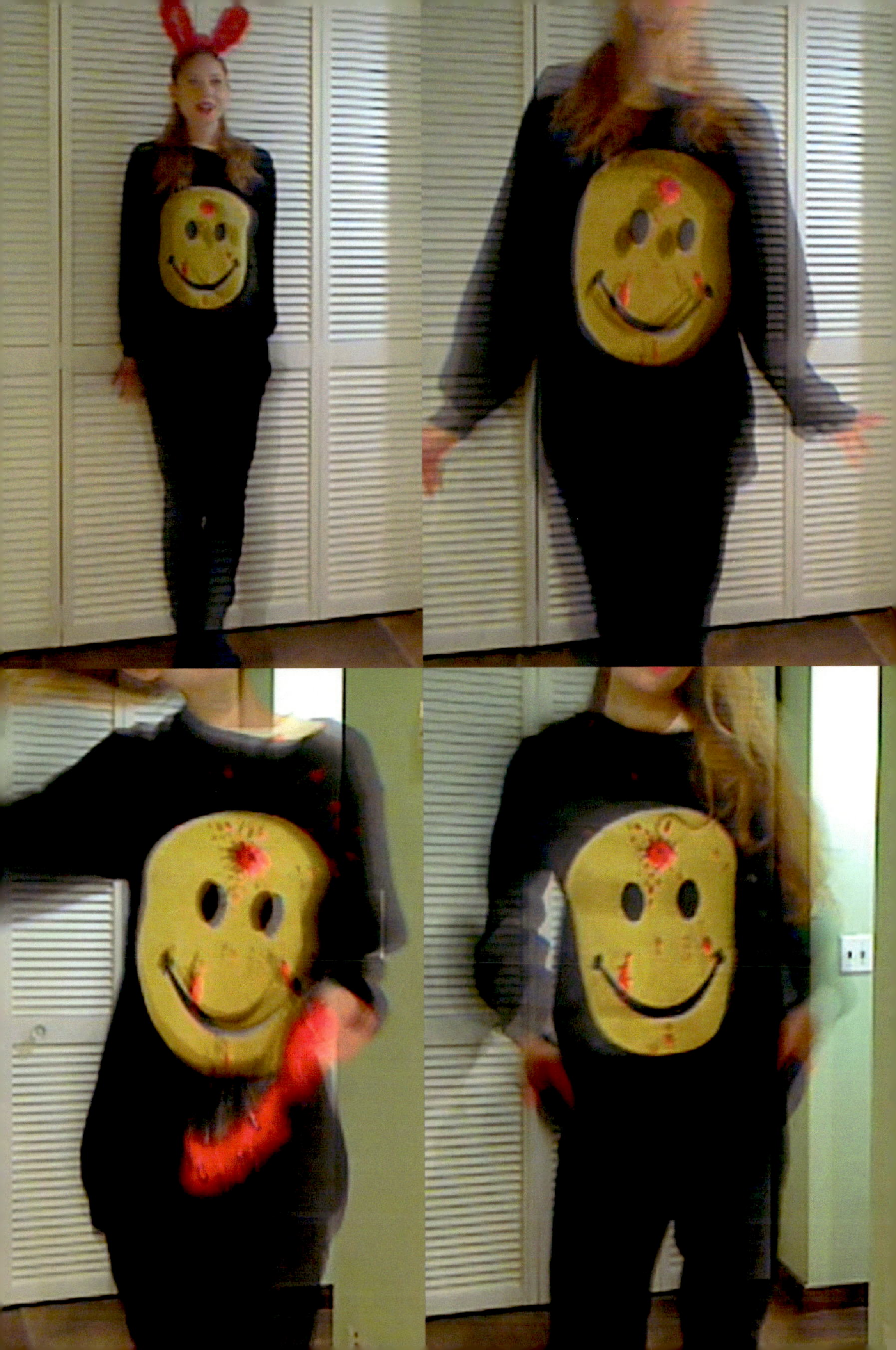

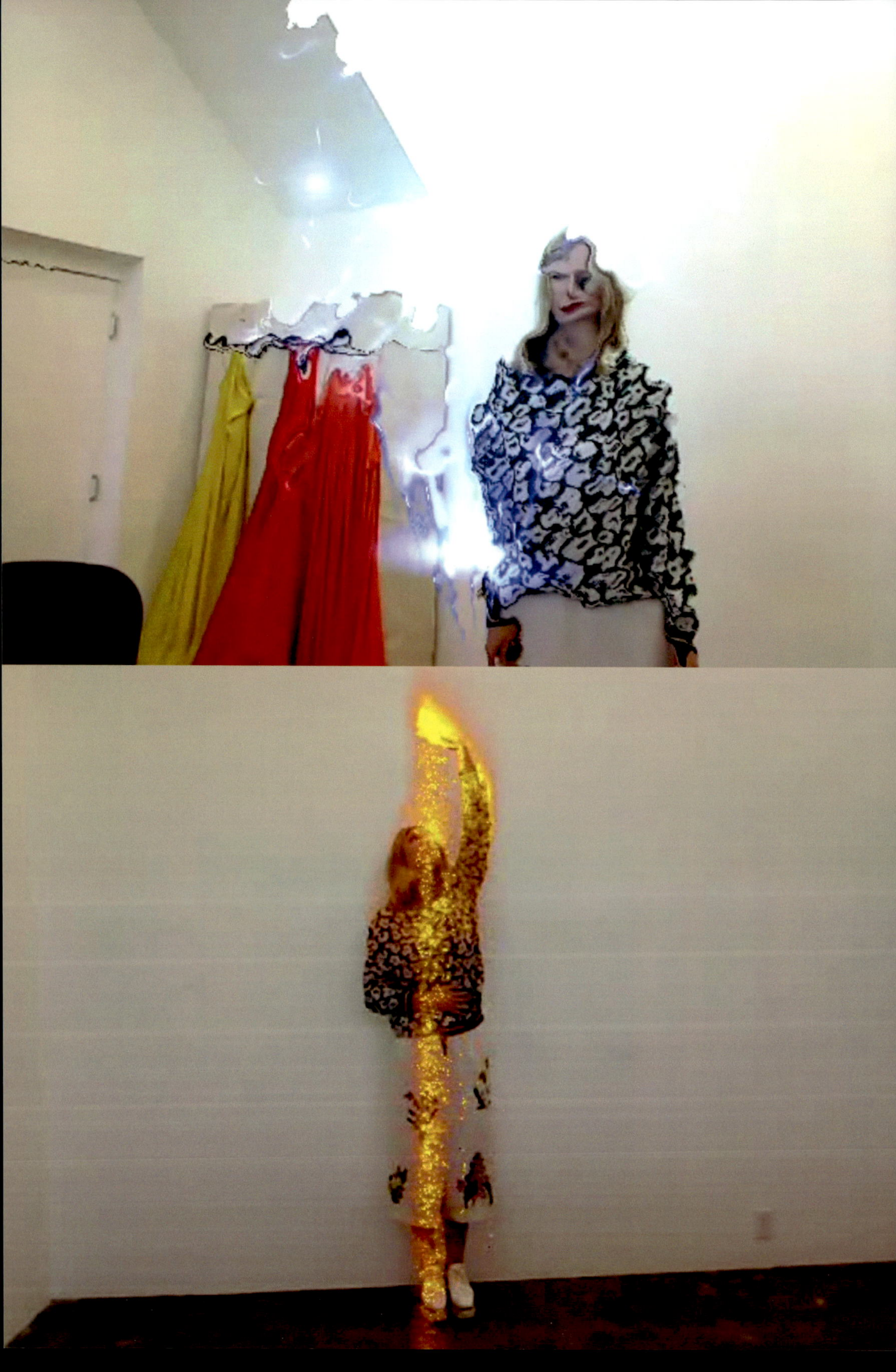

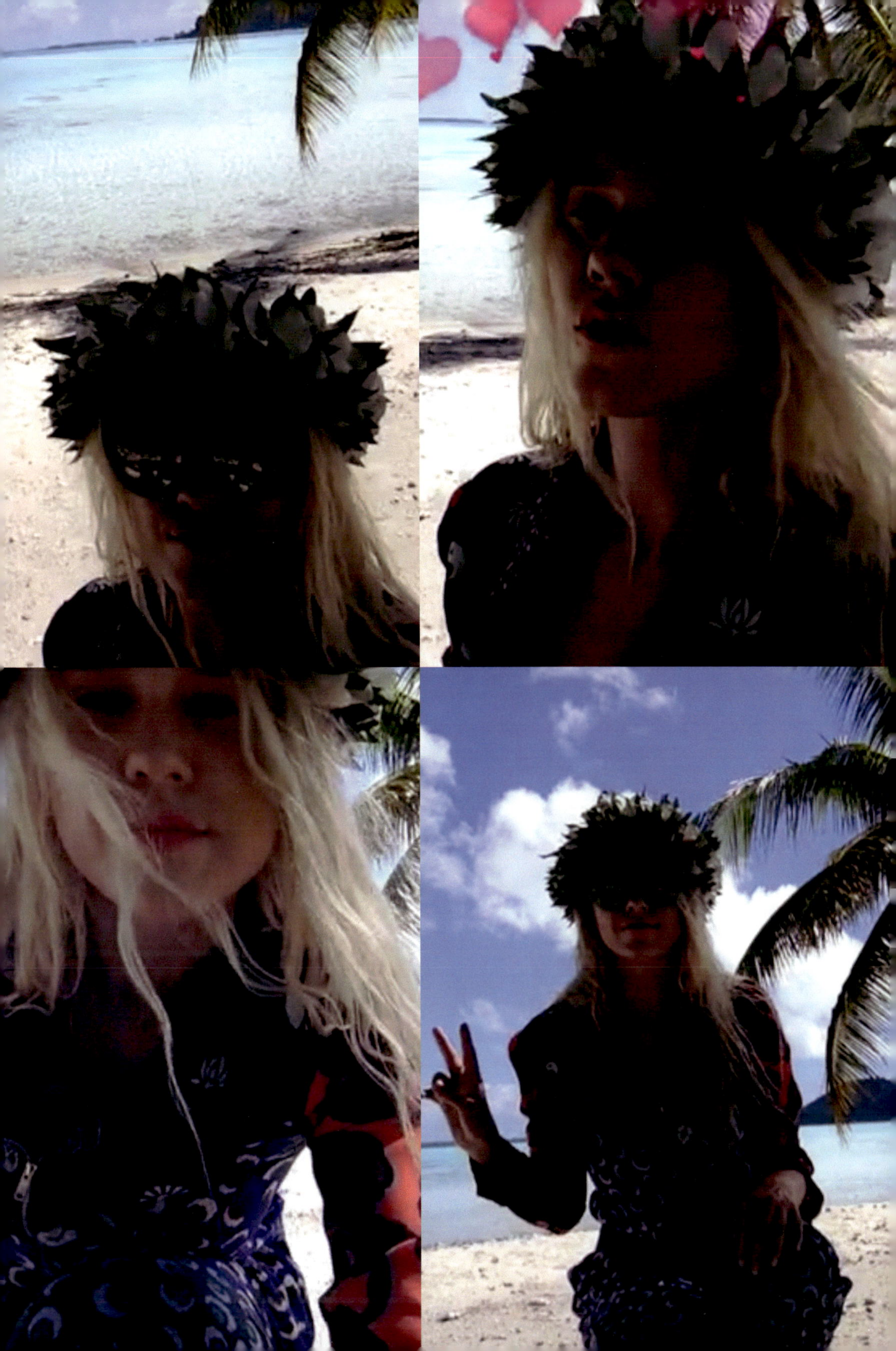

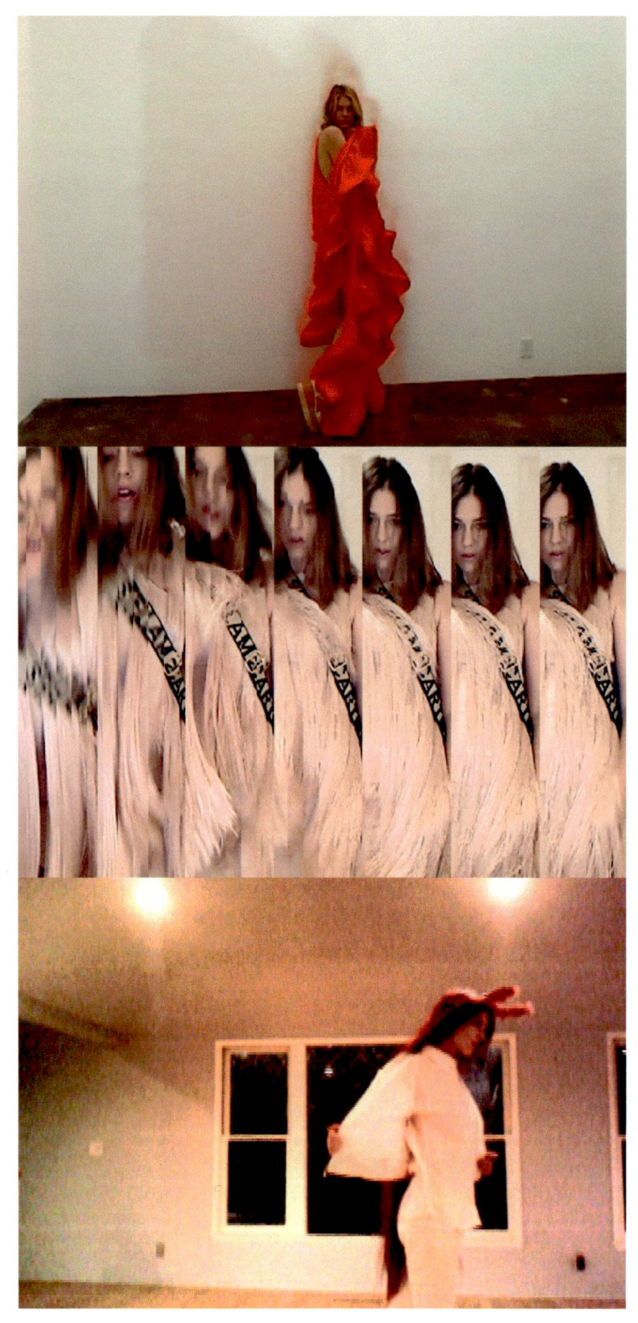

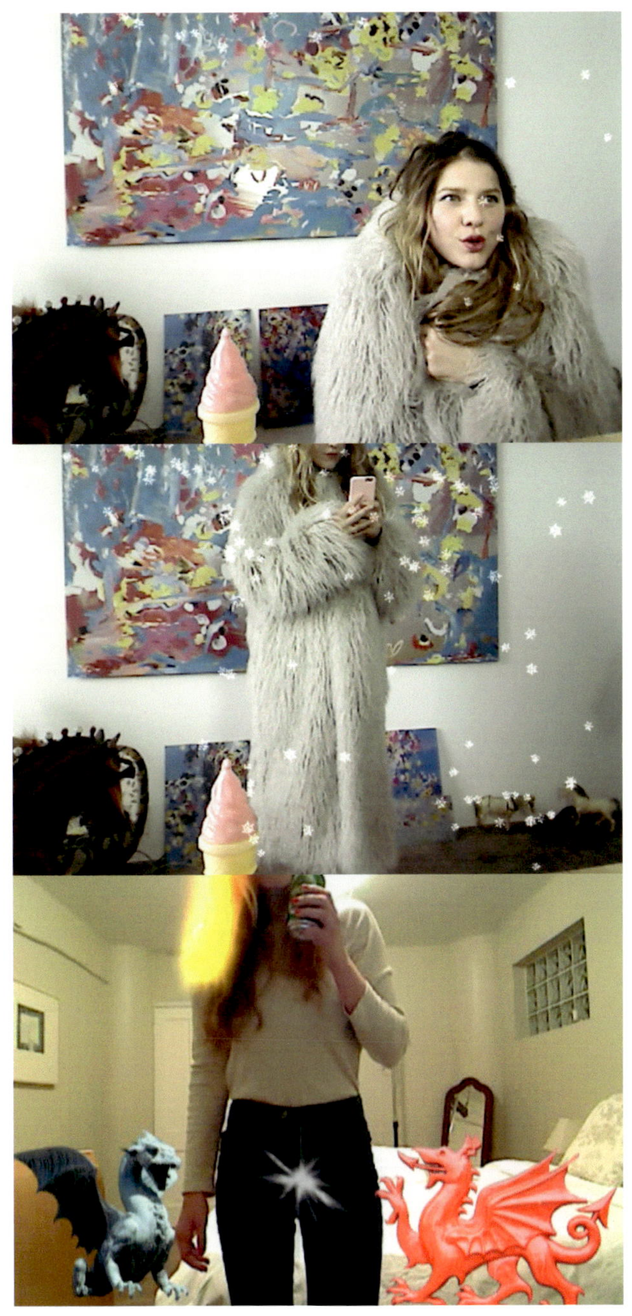

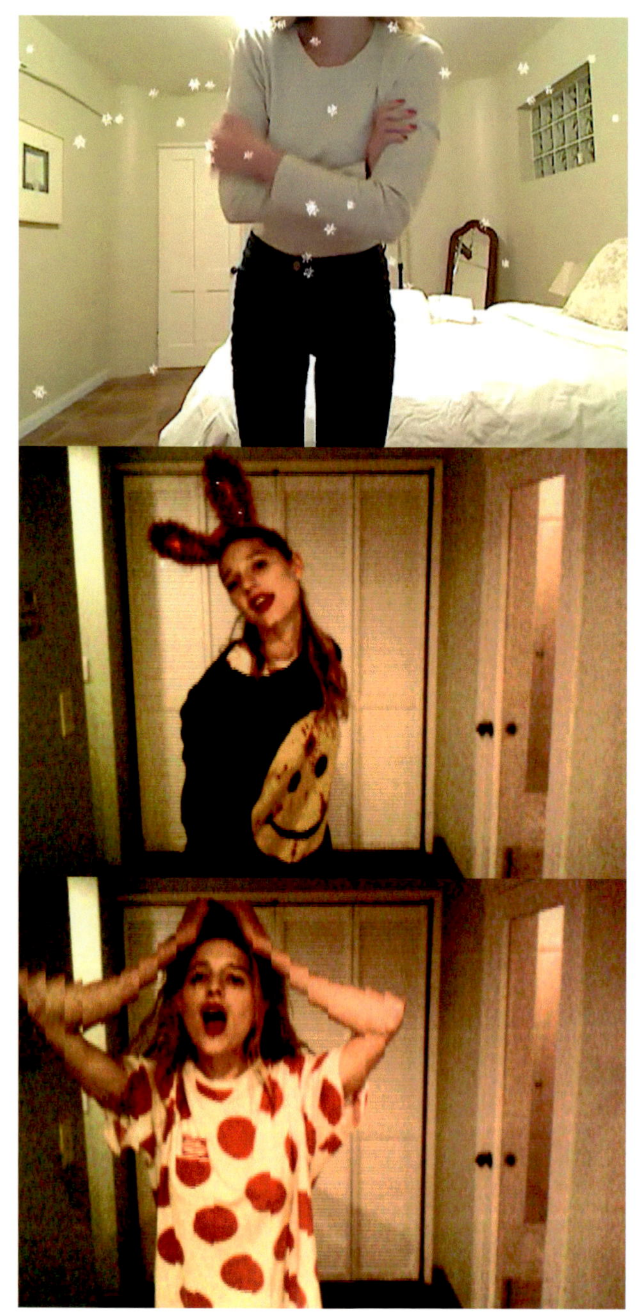

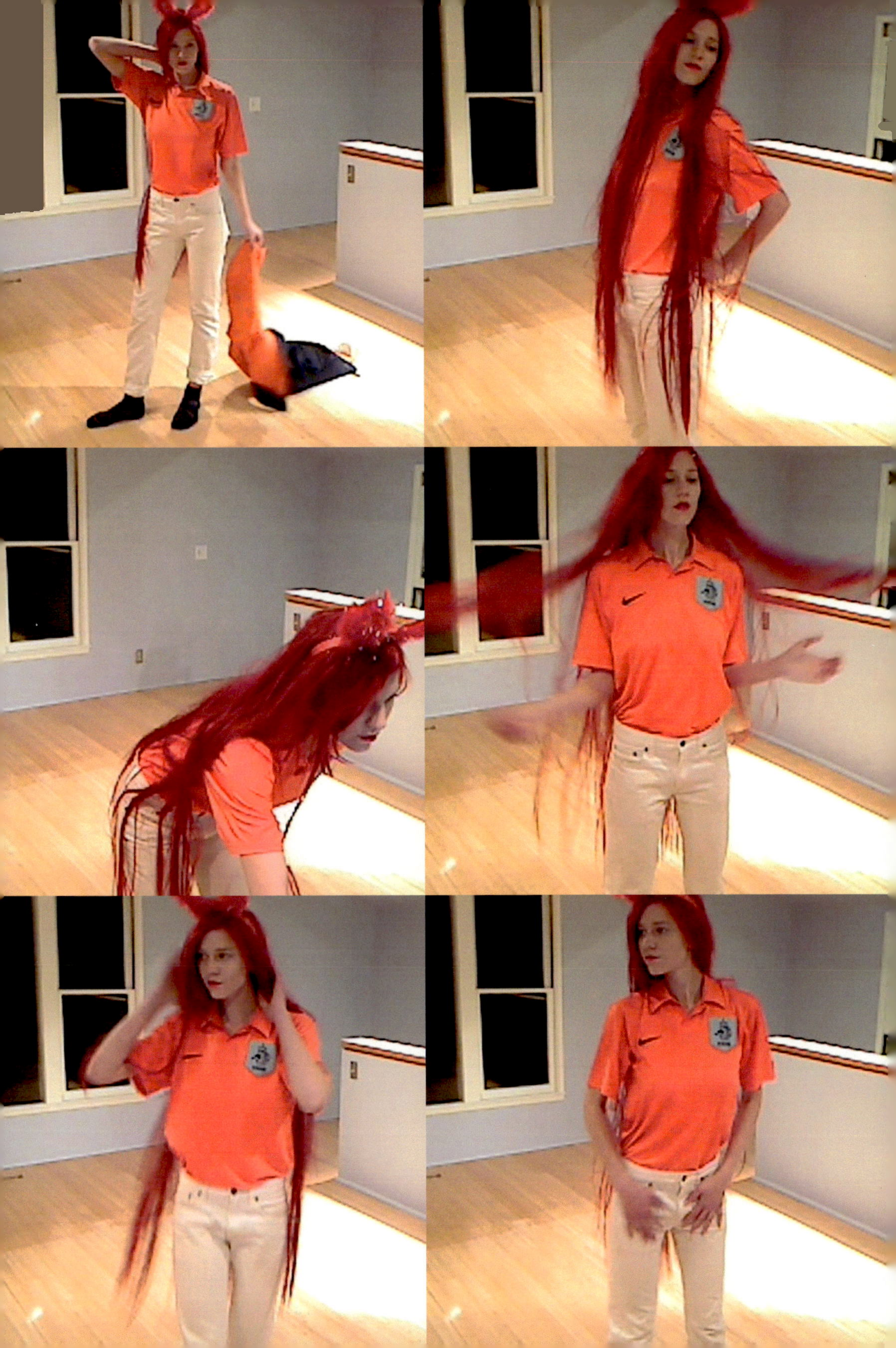

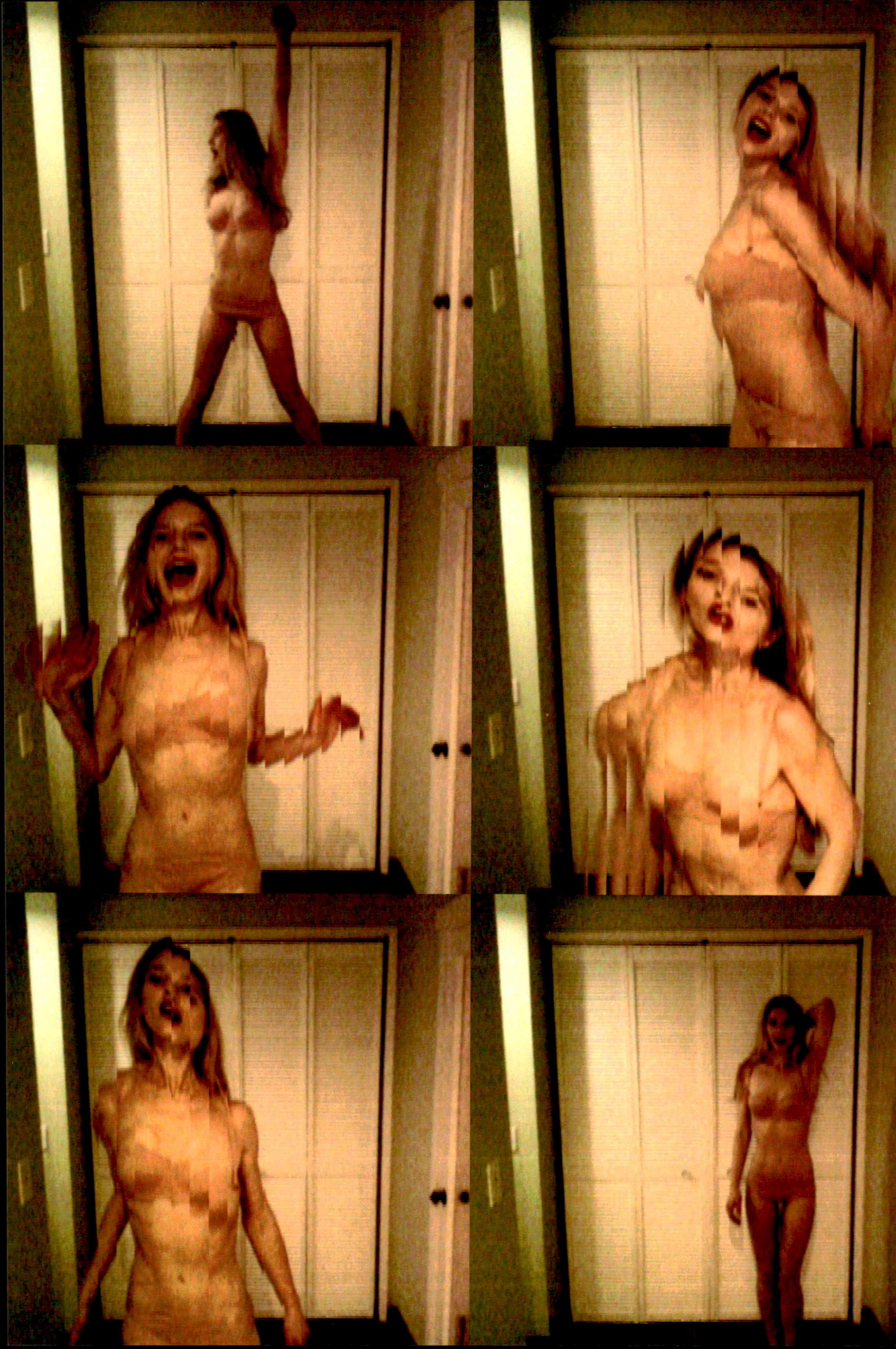

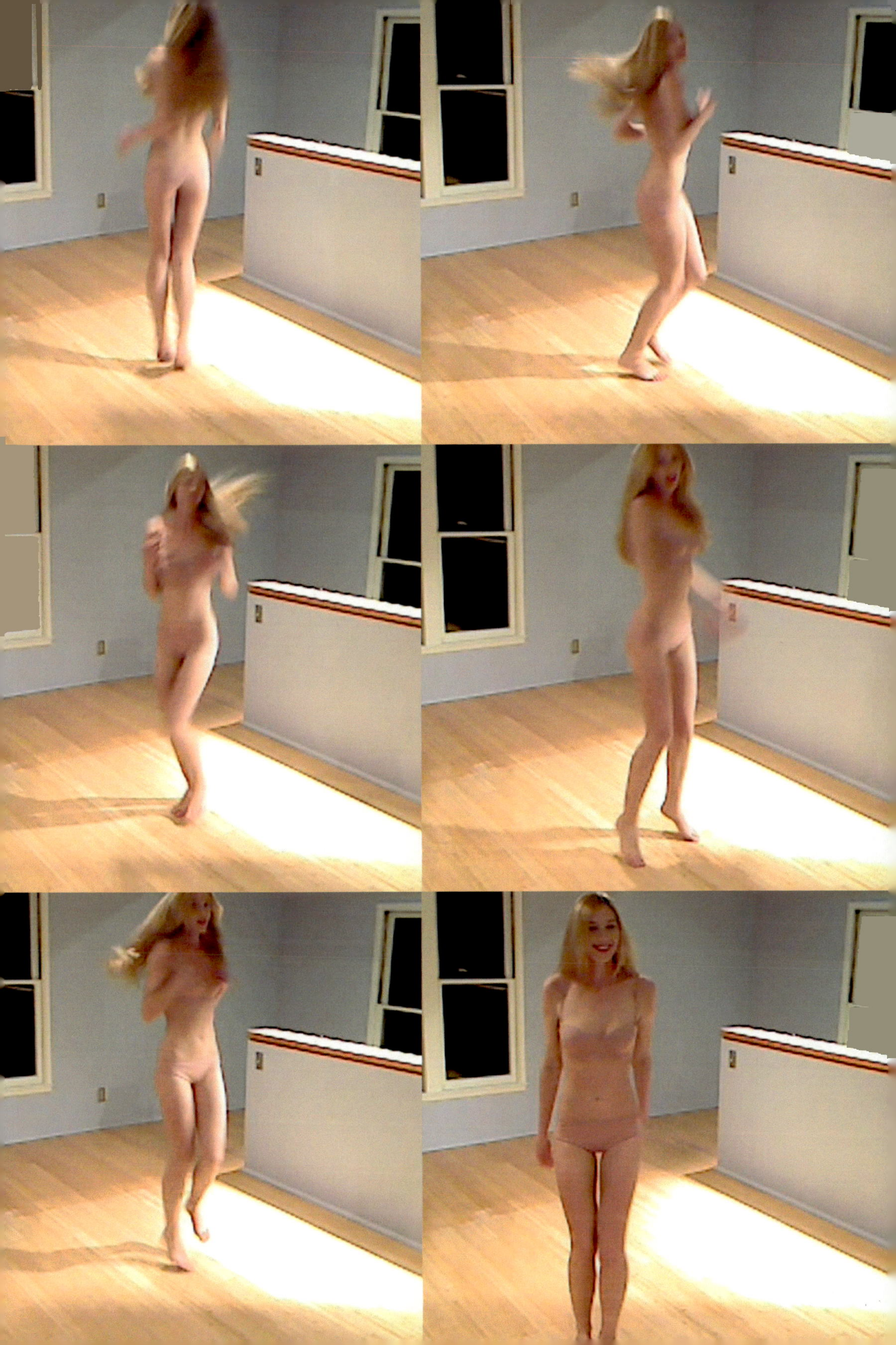

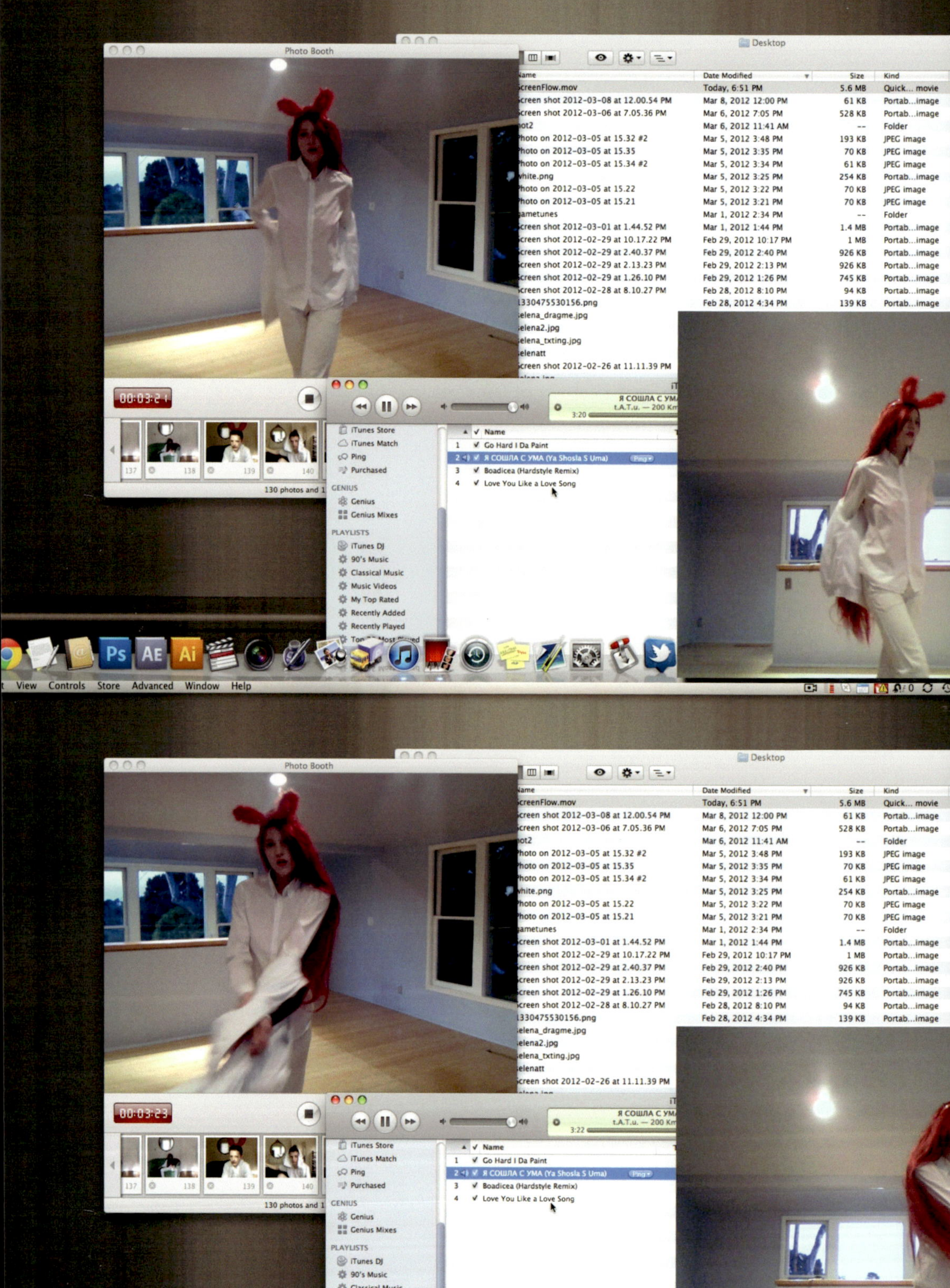

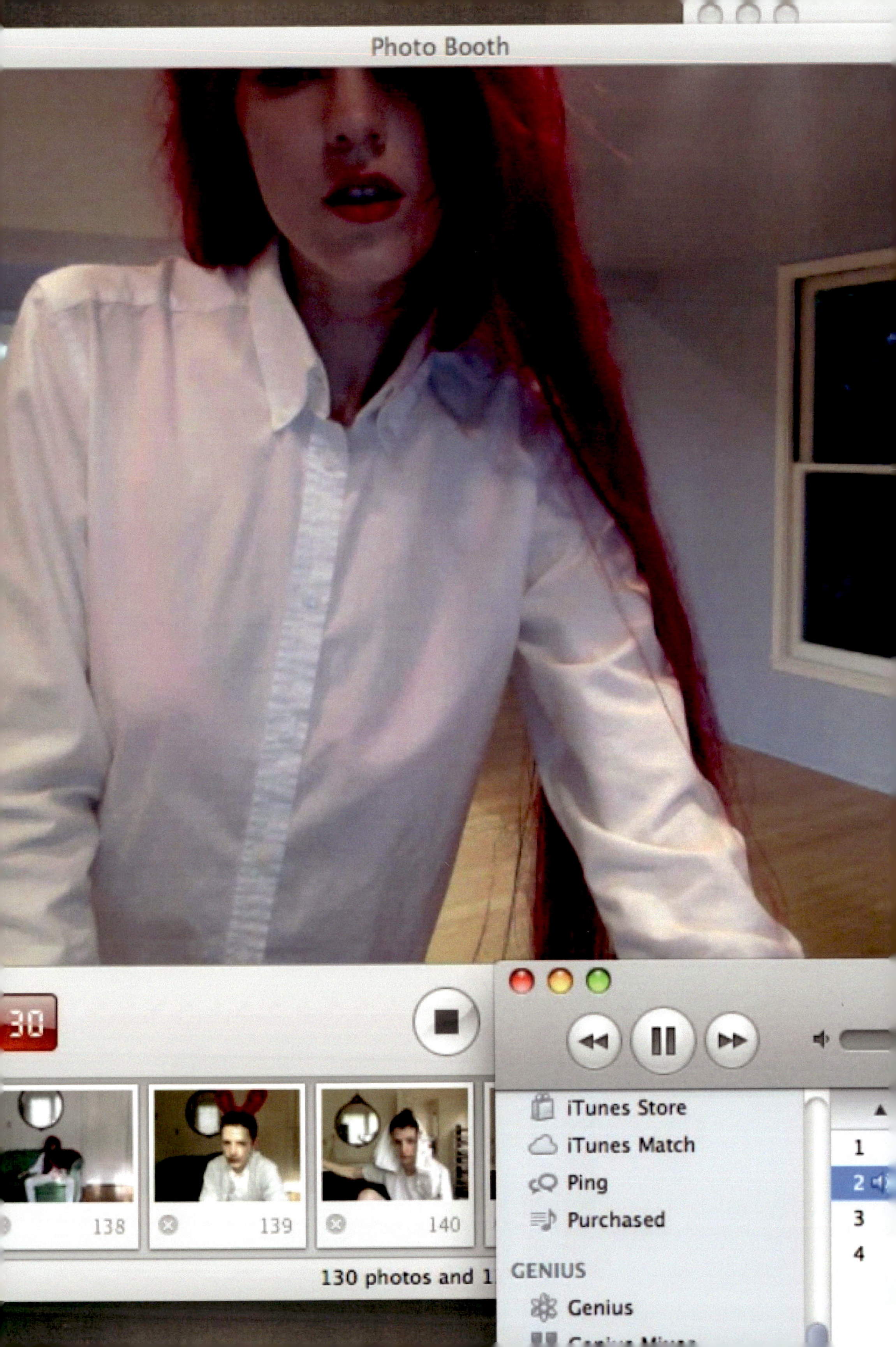

Photo Booth

30

138   139   140

130 photos and 1

iTunes Store
iTunes Match
Ping
Purchased

GENIUS

Genius

1
2
3
4

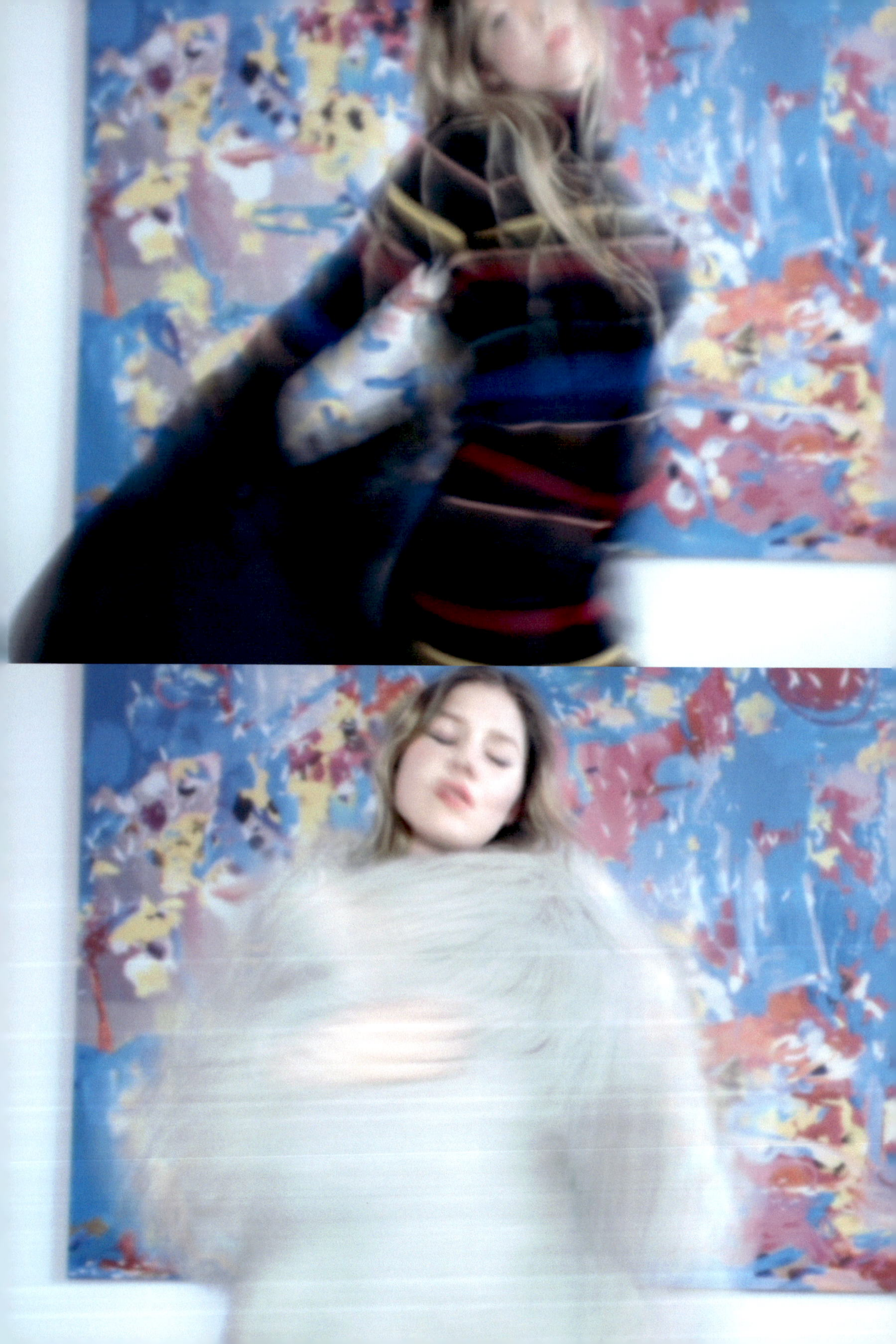

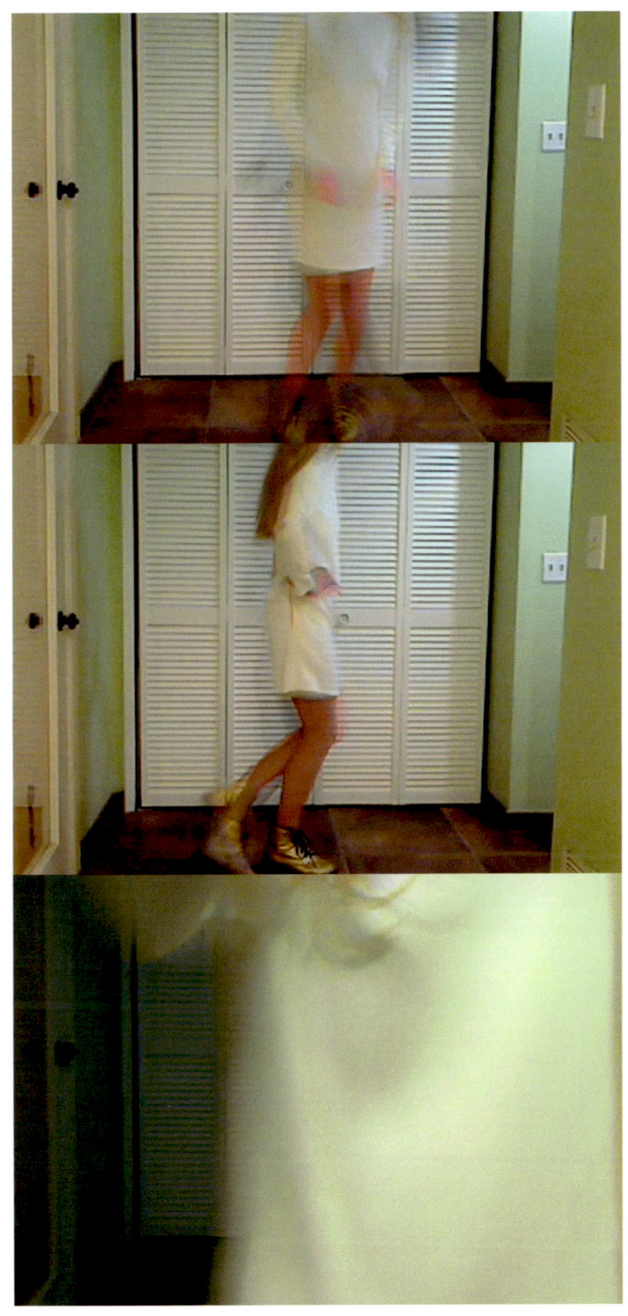

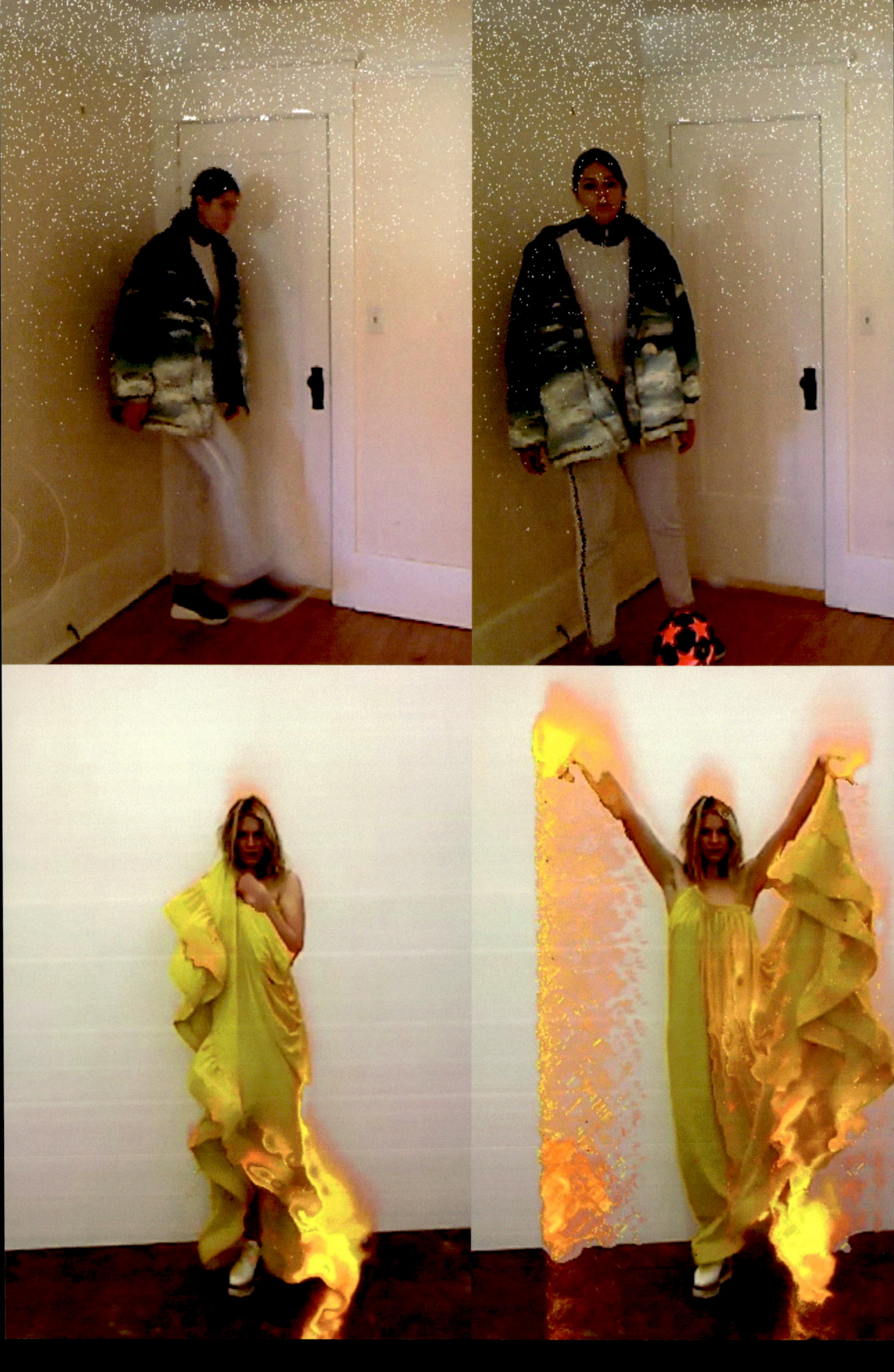

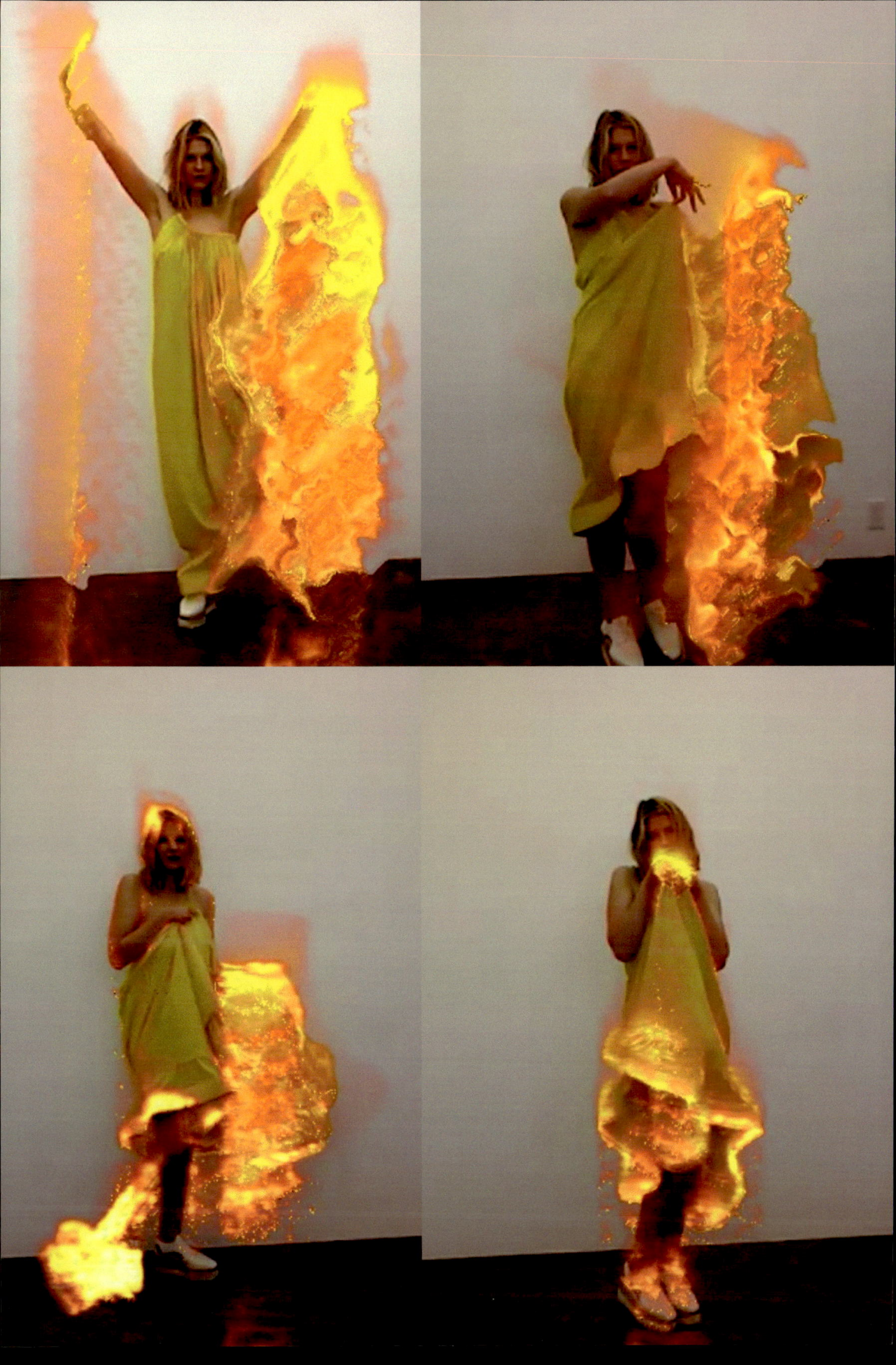

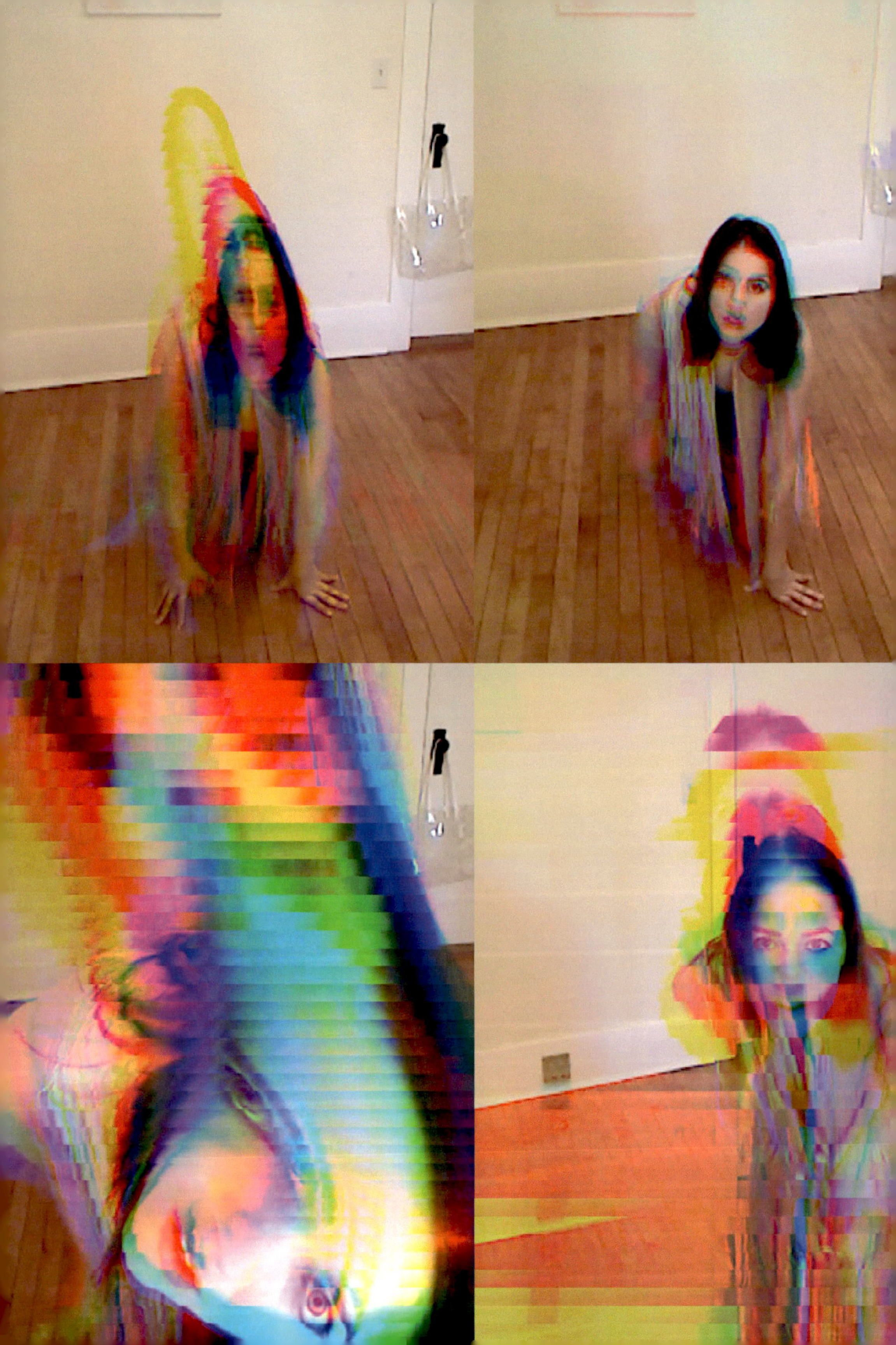

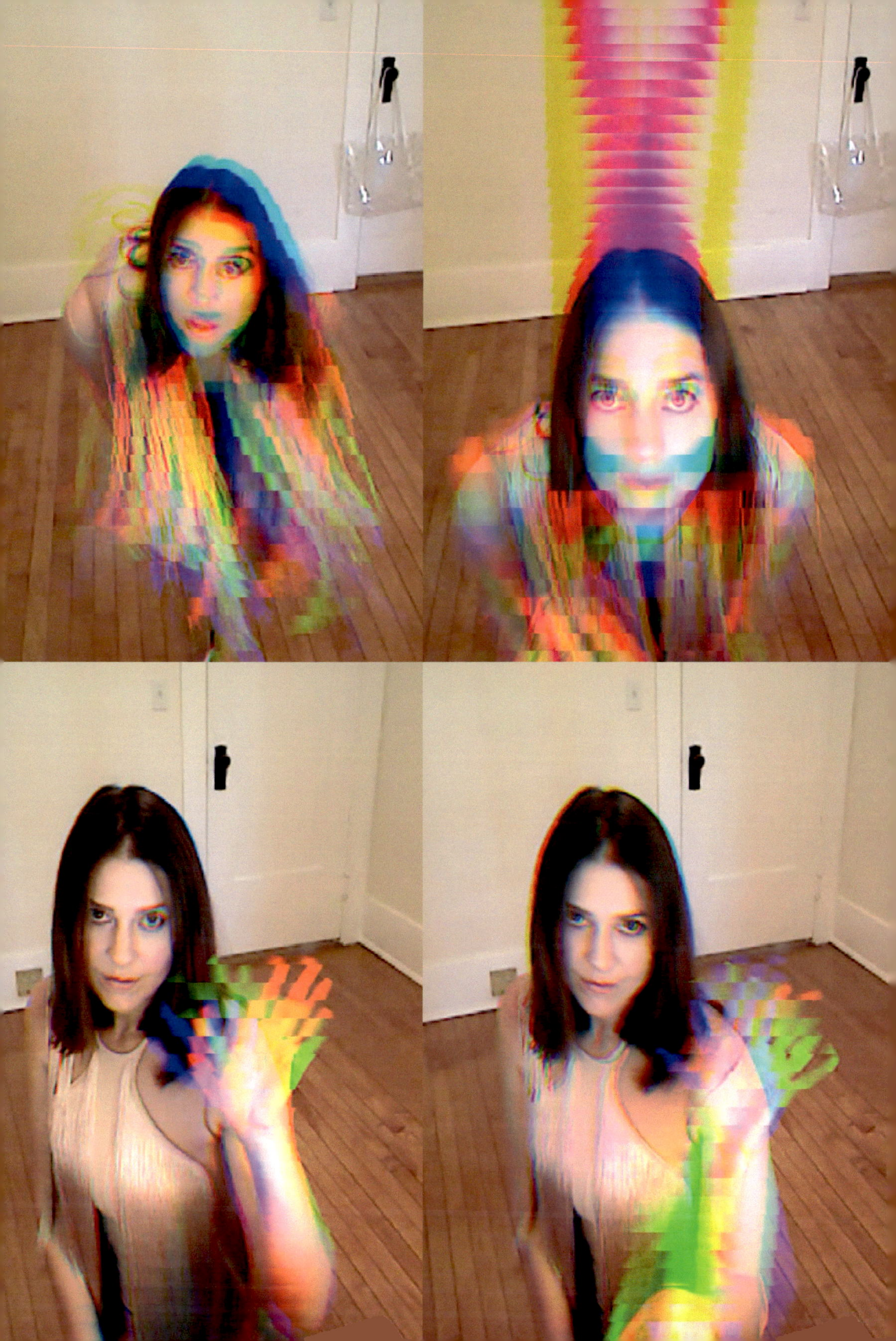

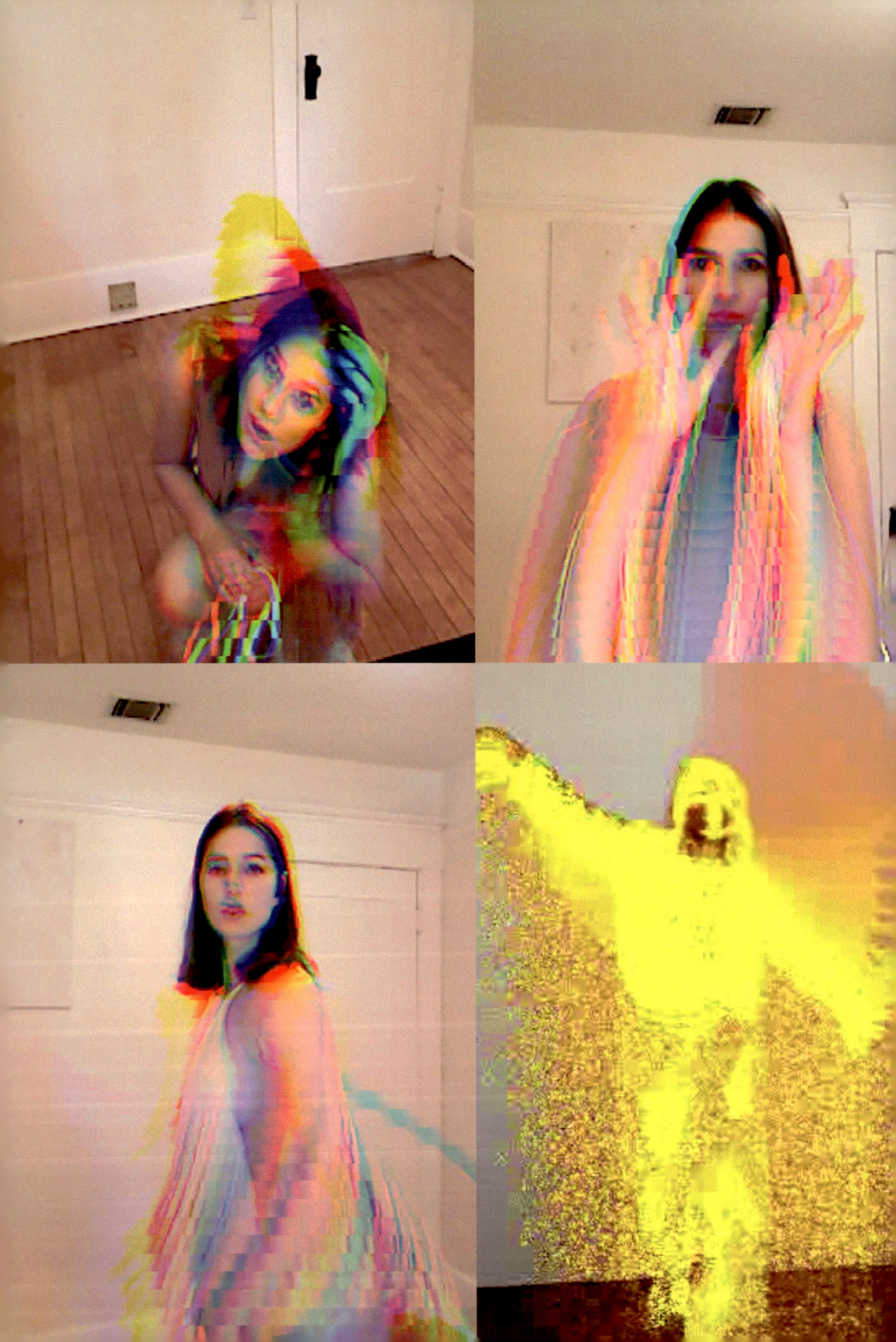

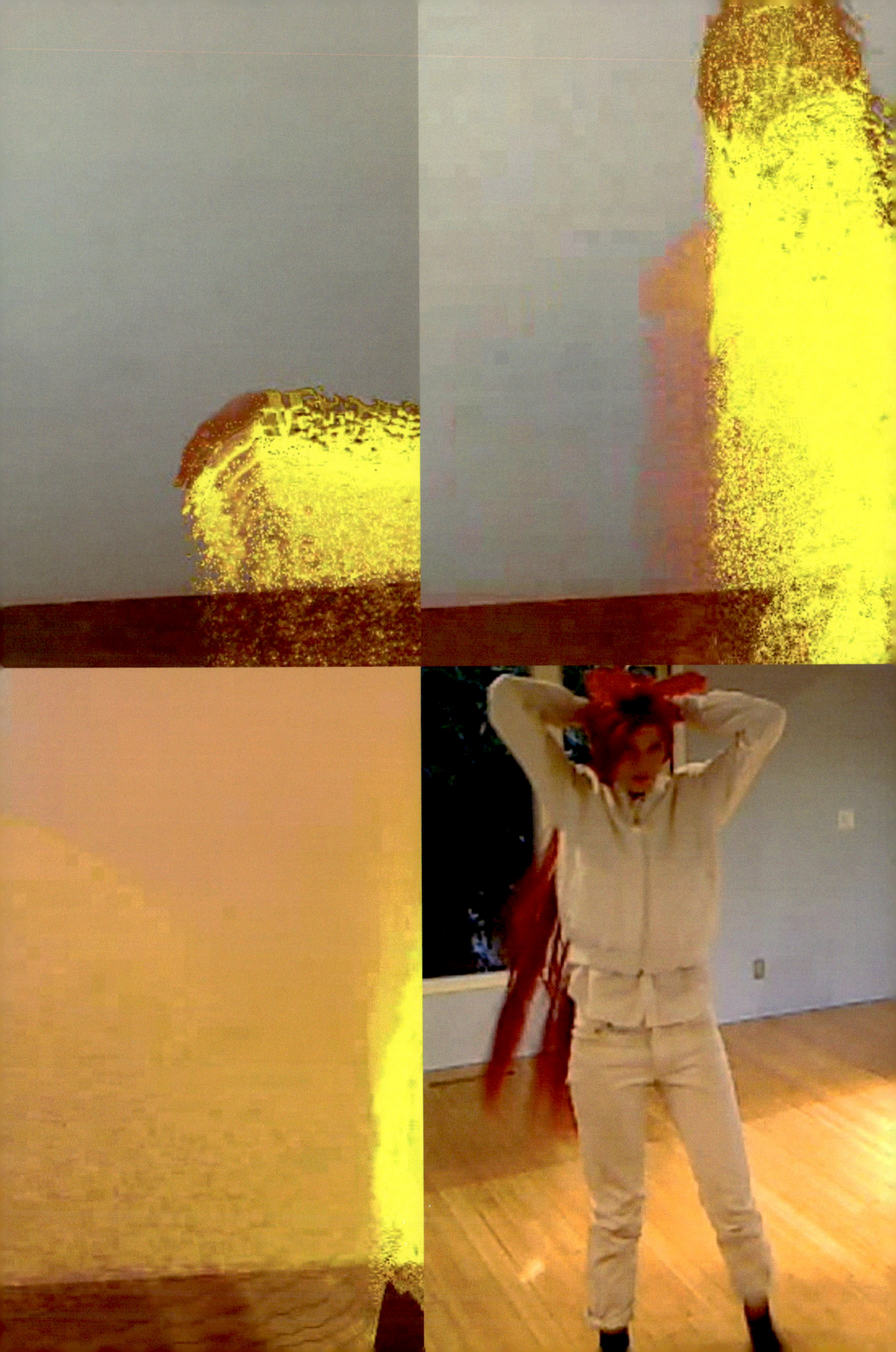

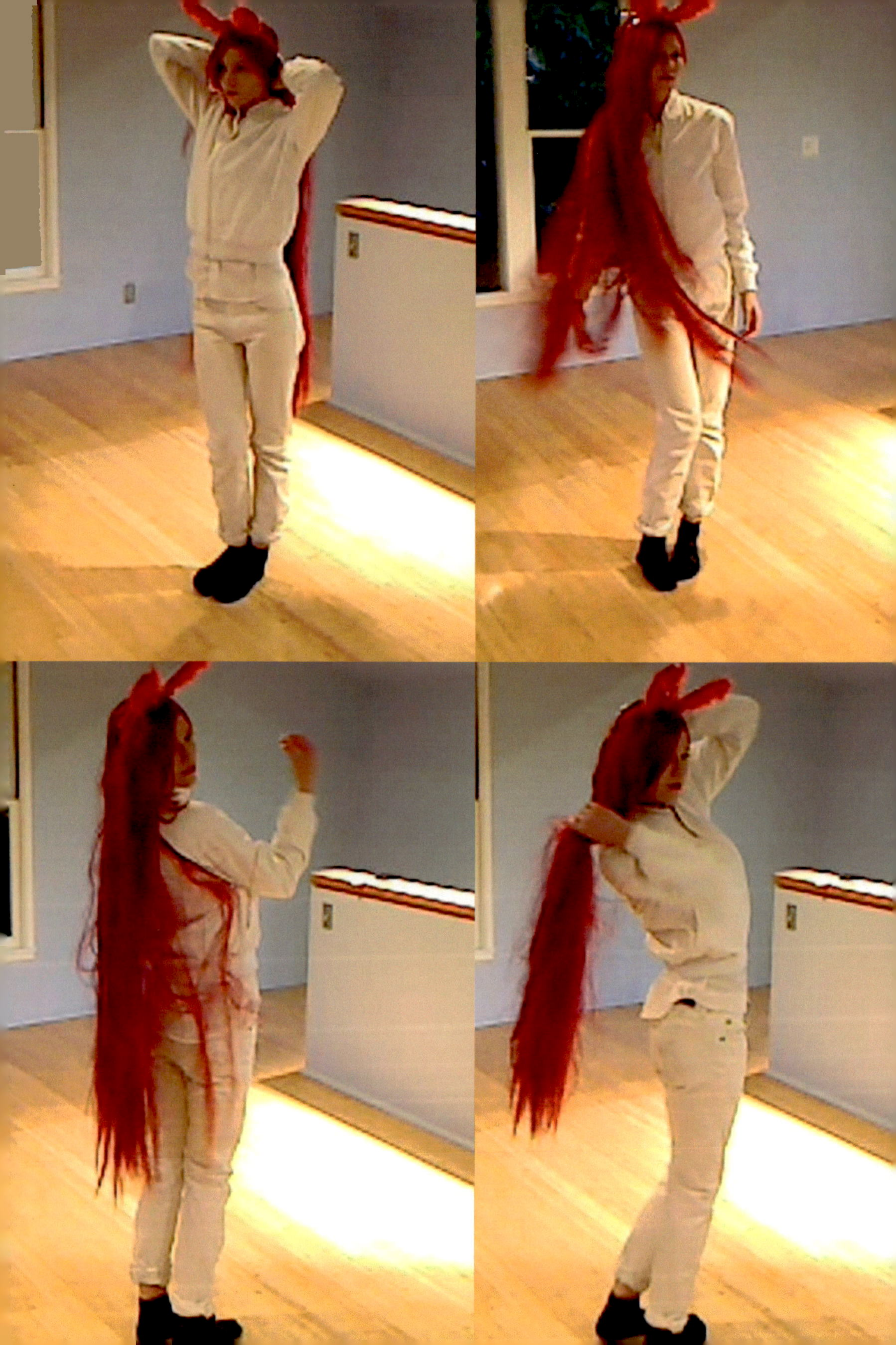

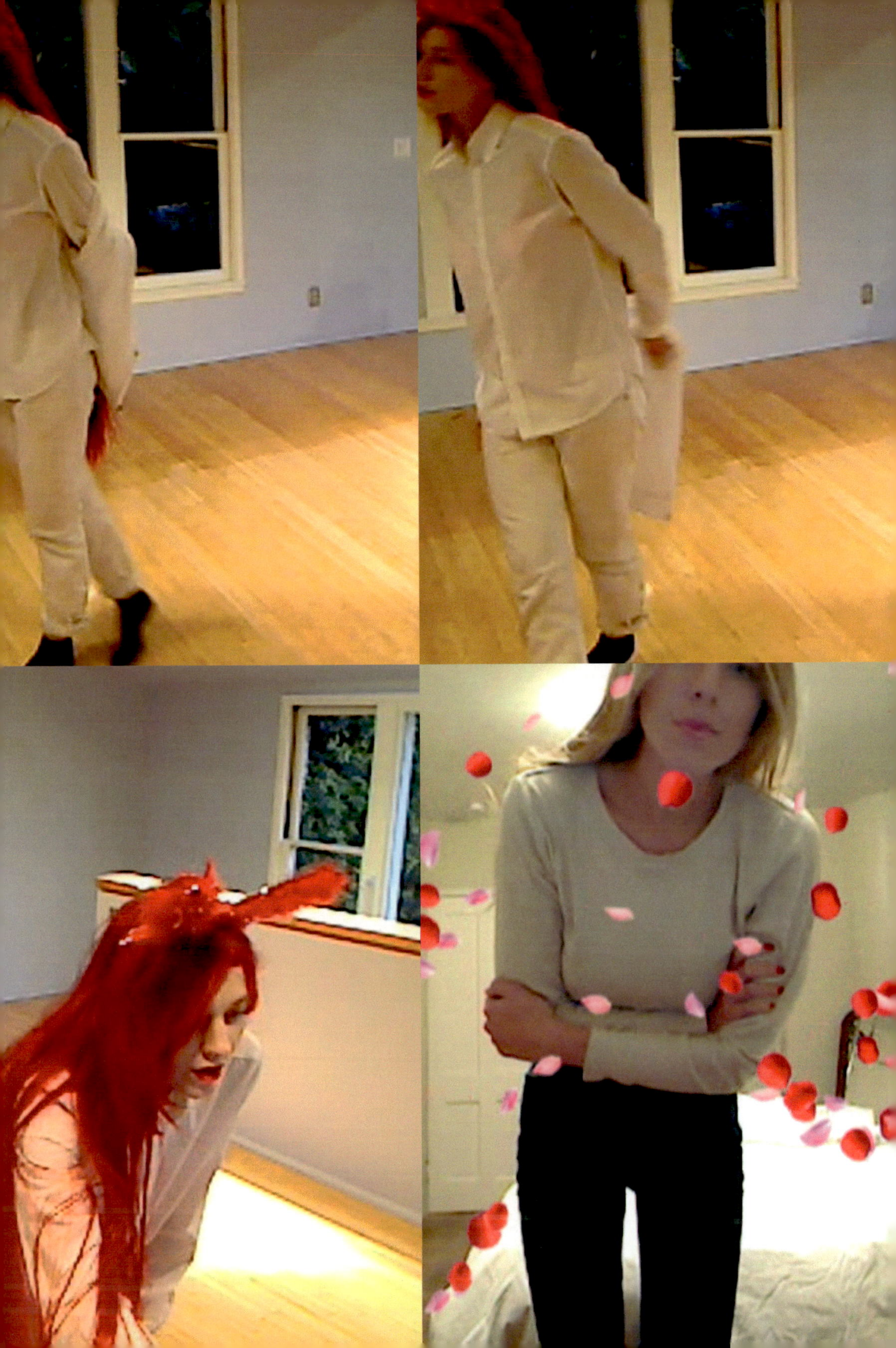

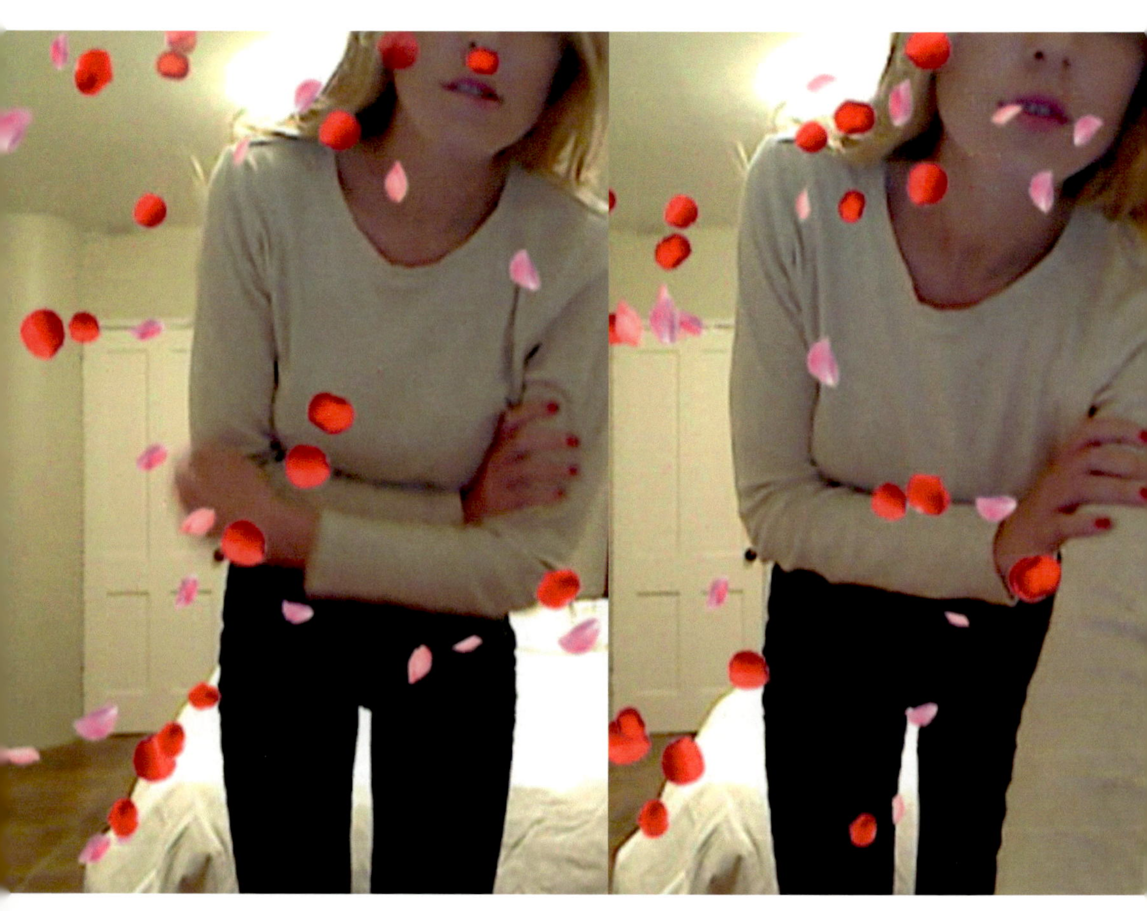

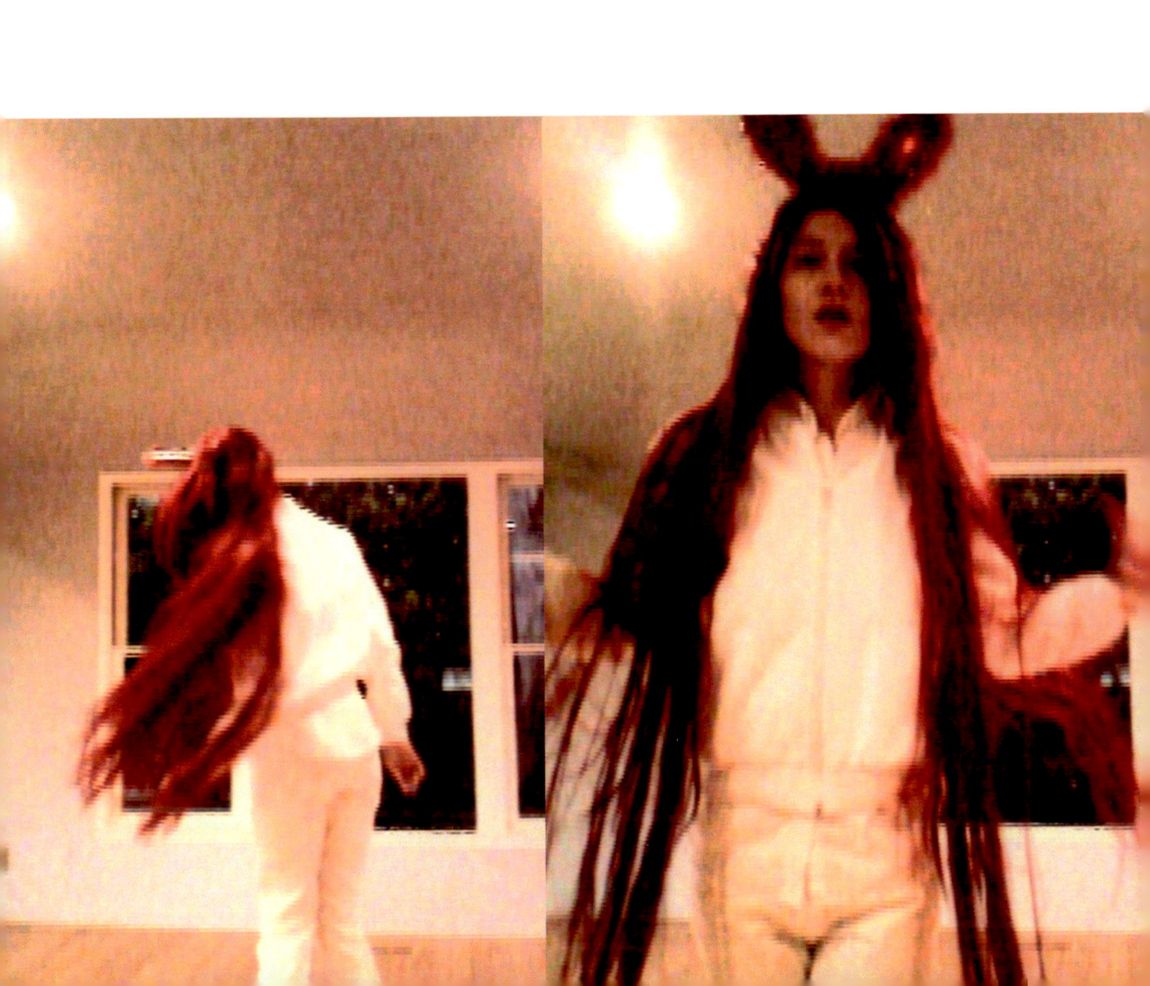

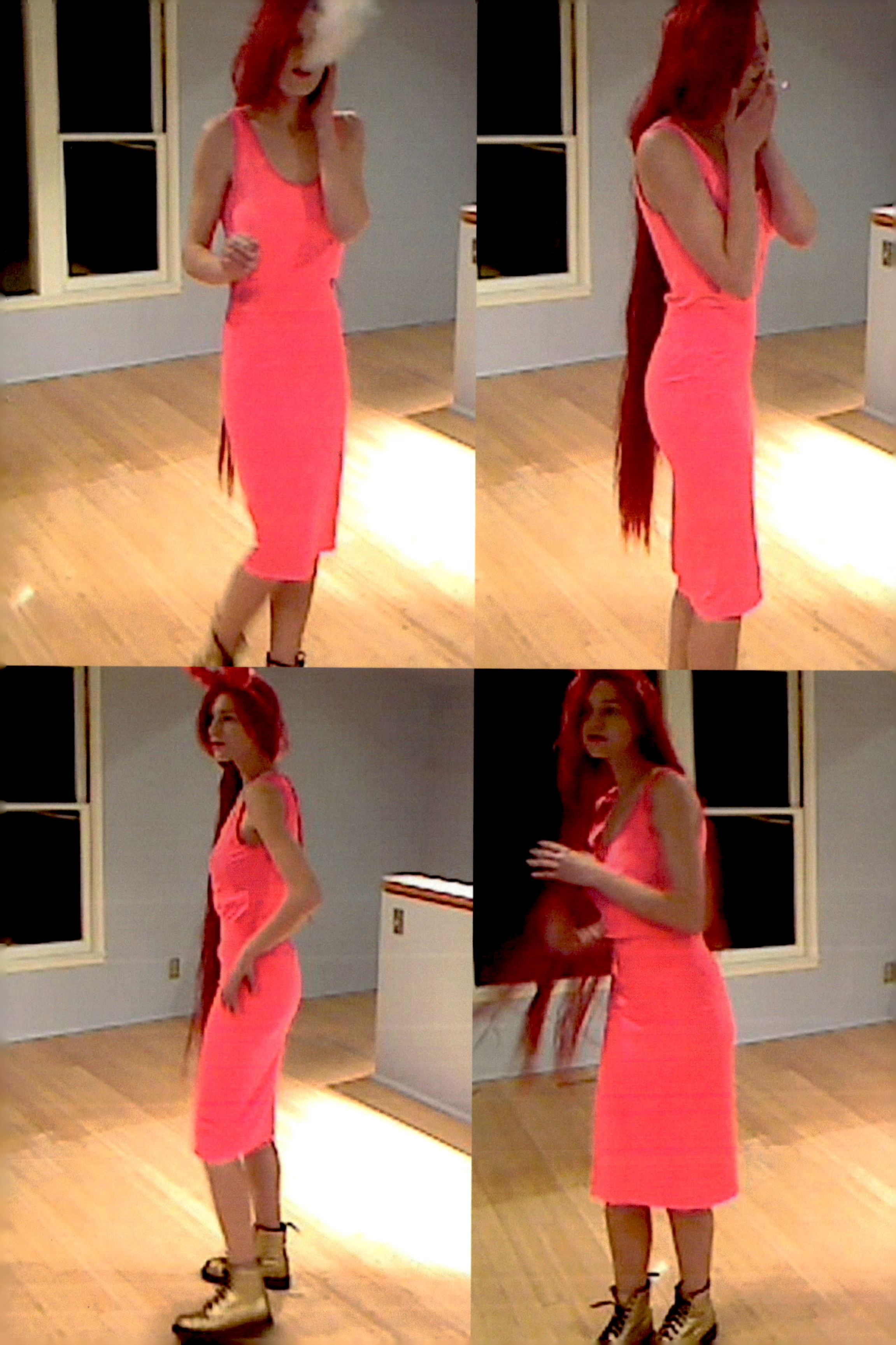

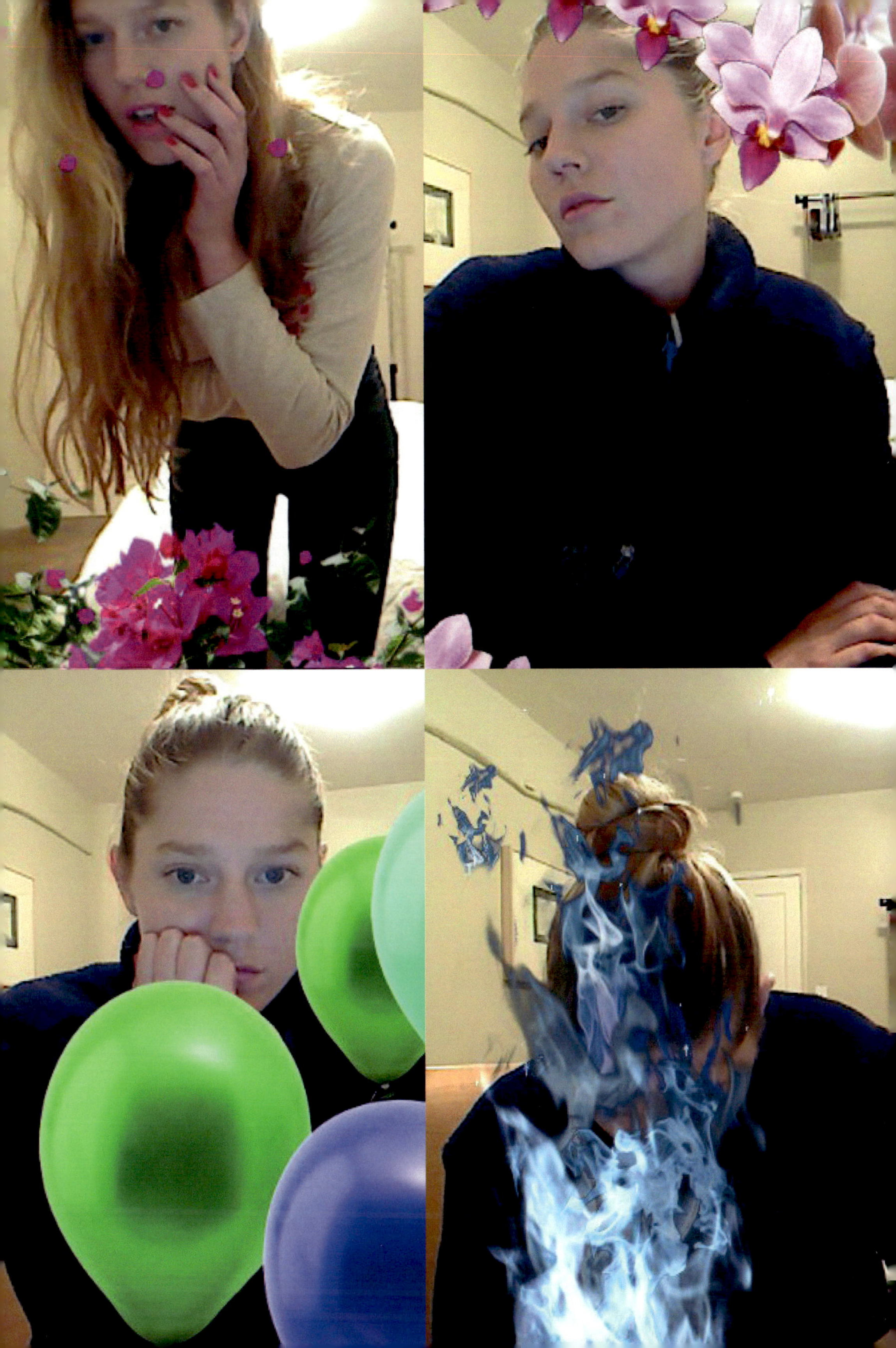

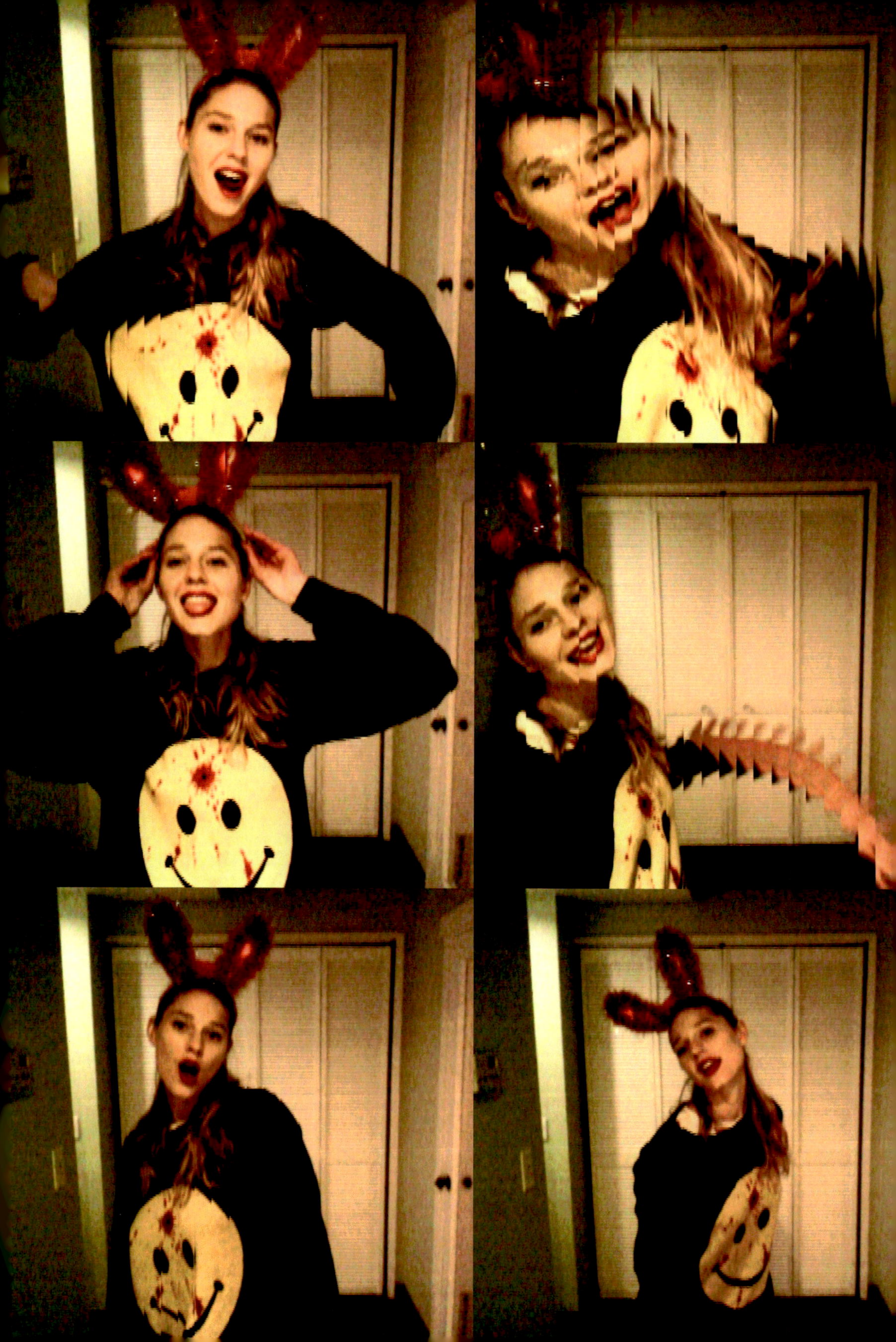

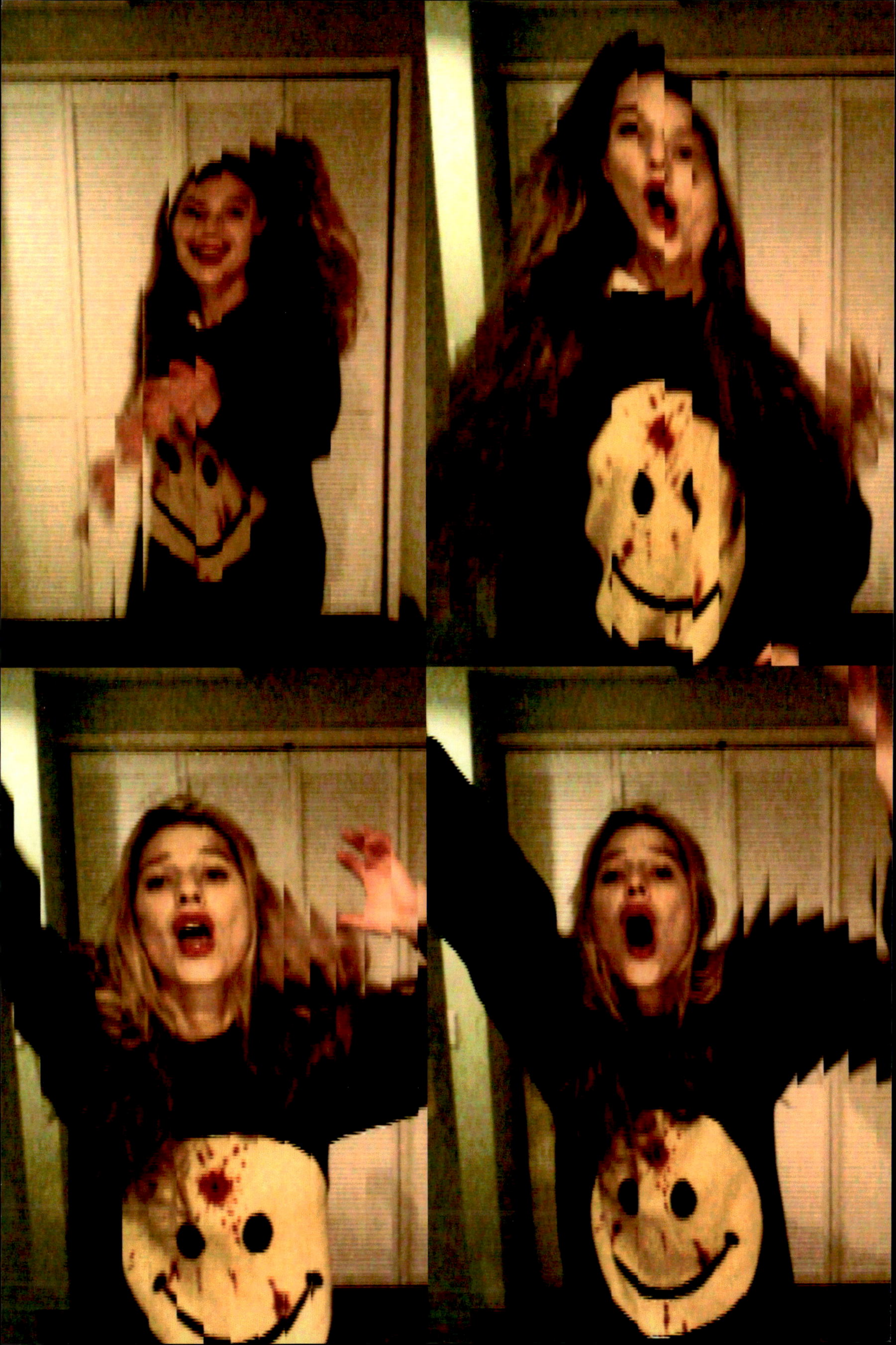

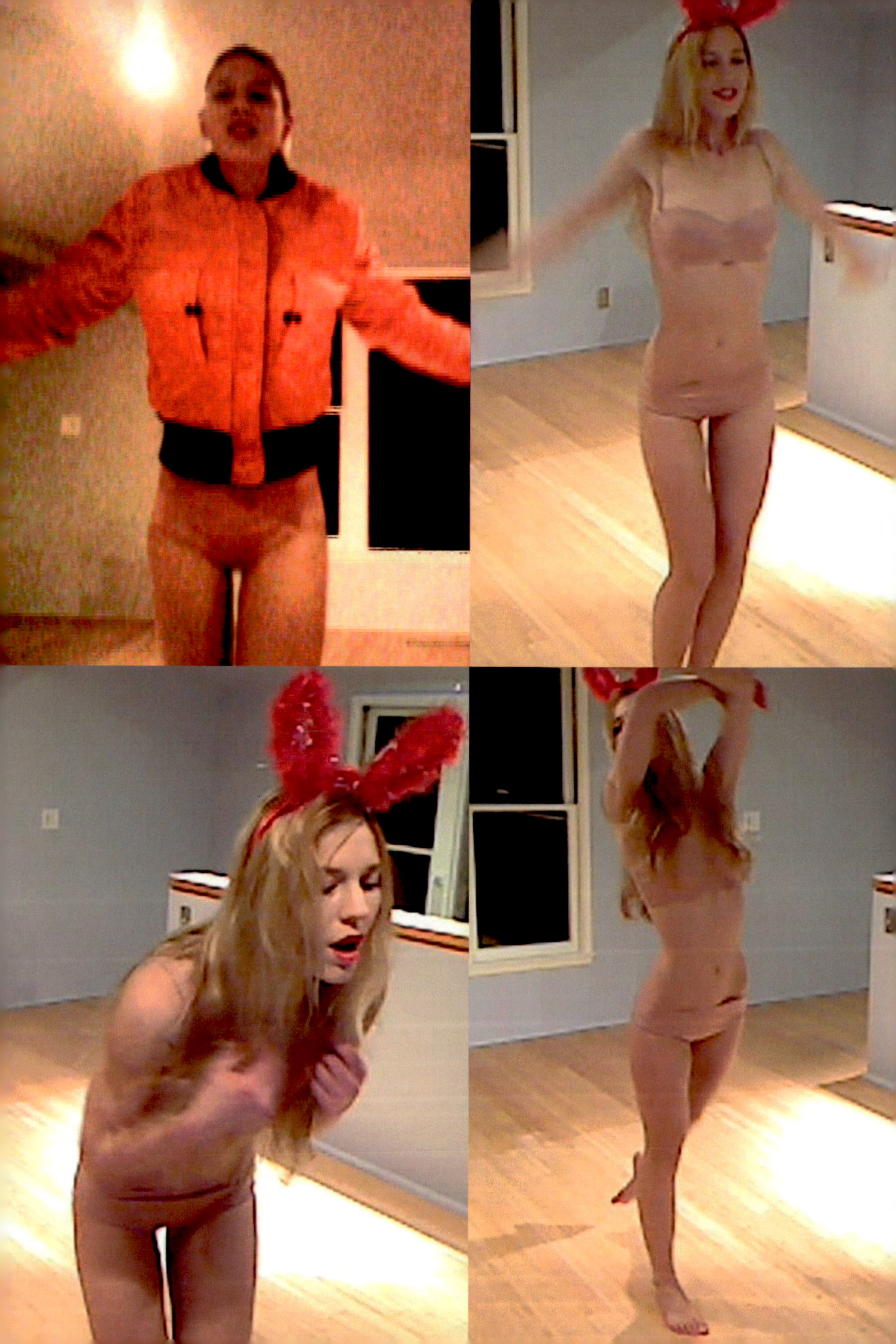

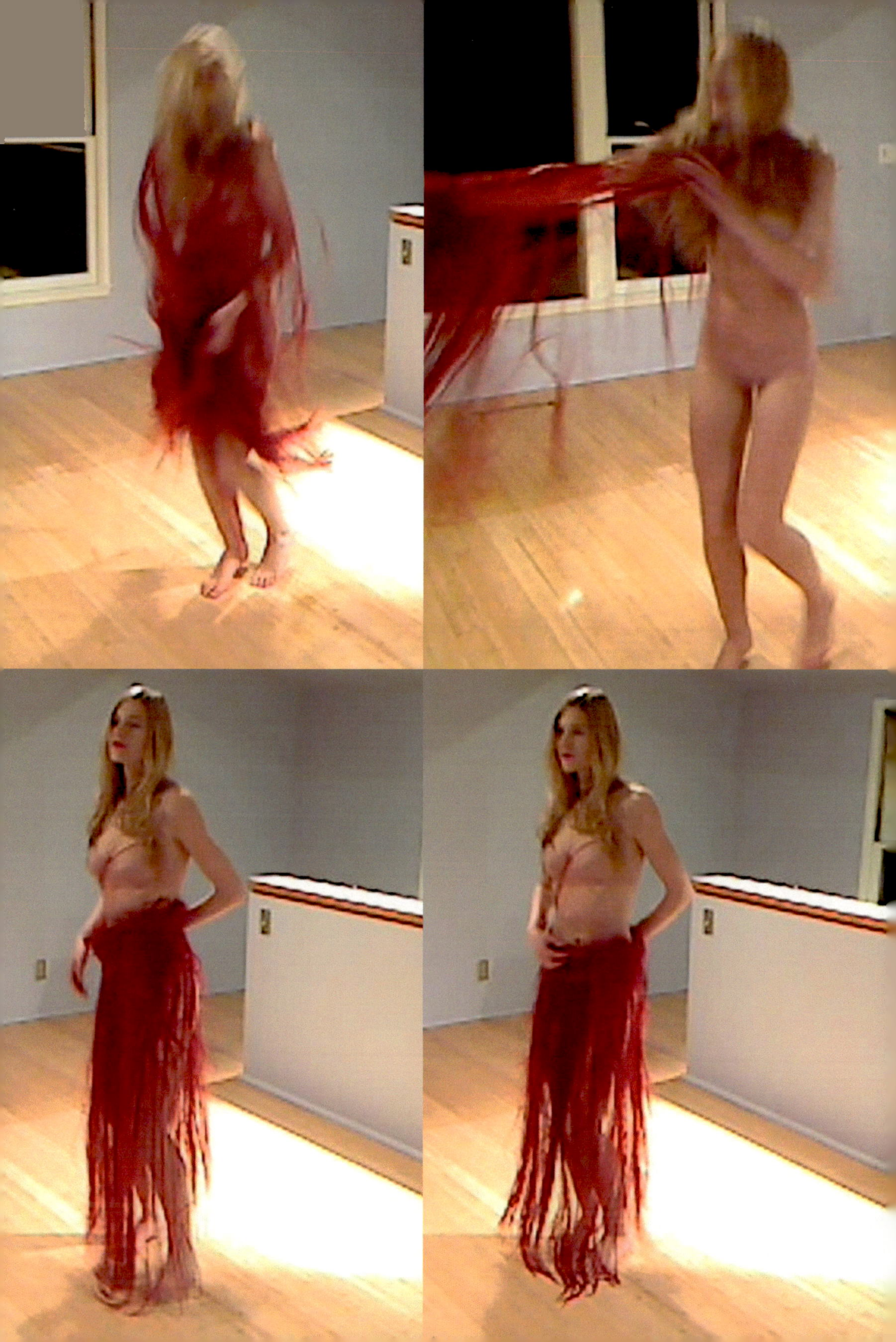

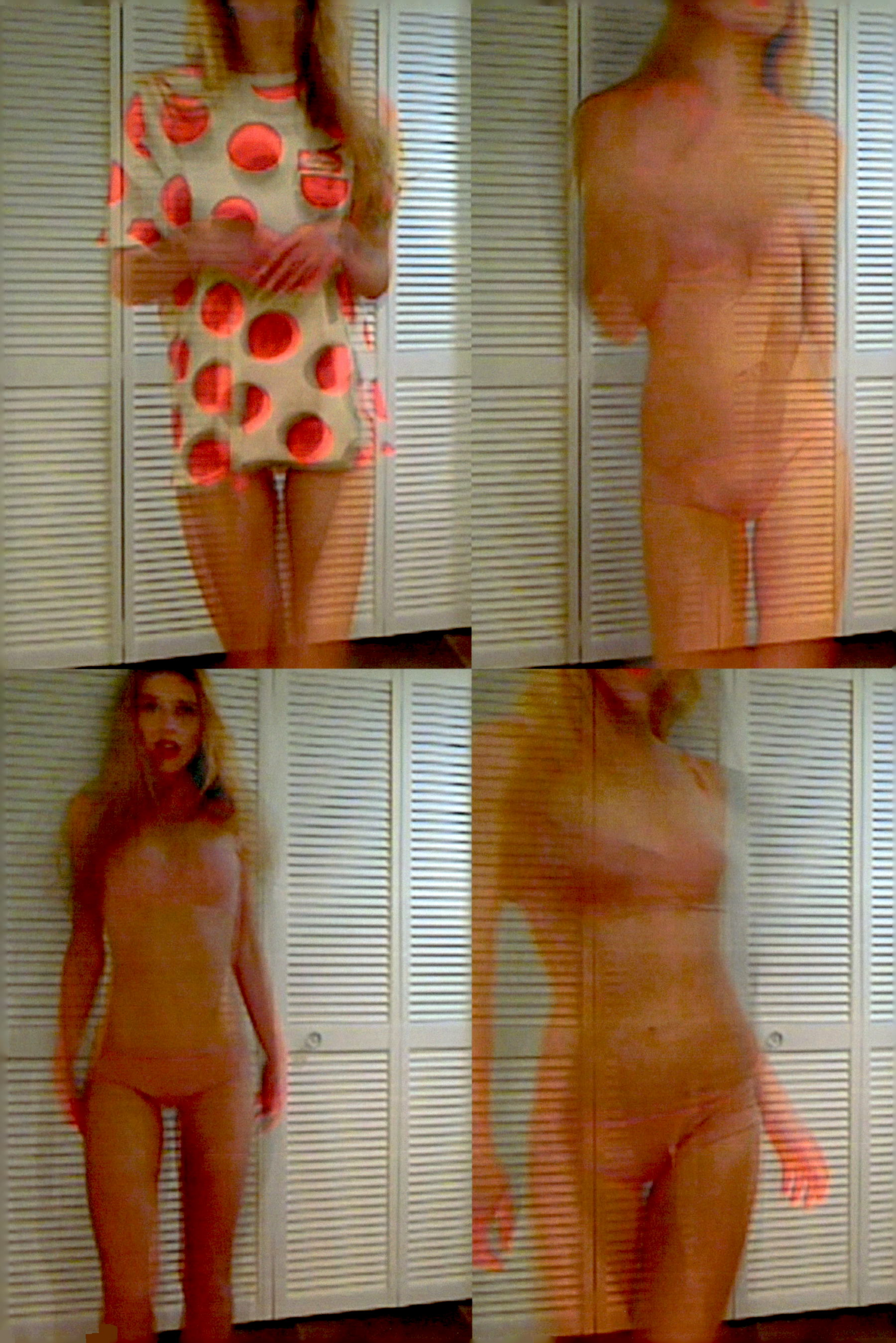

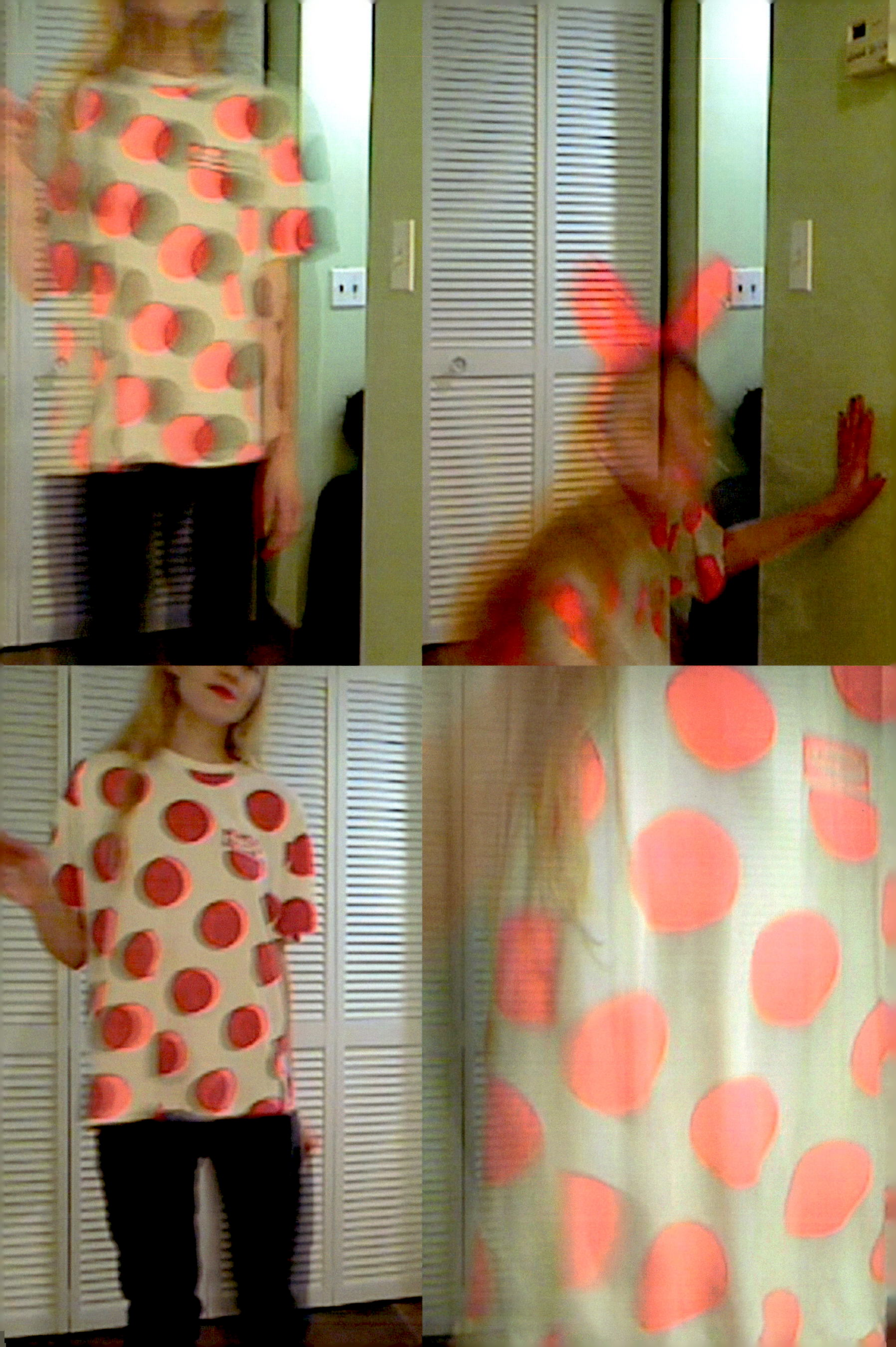

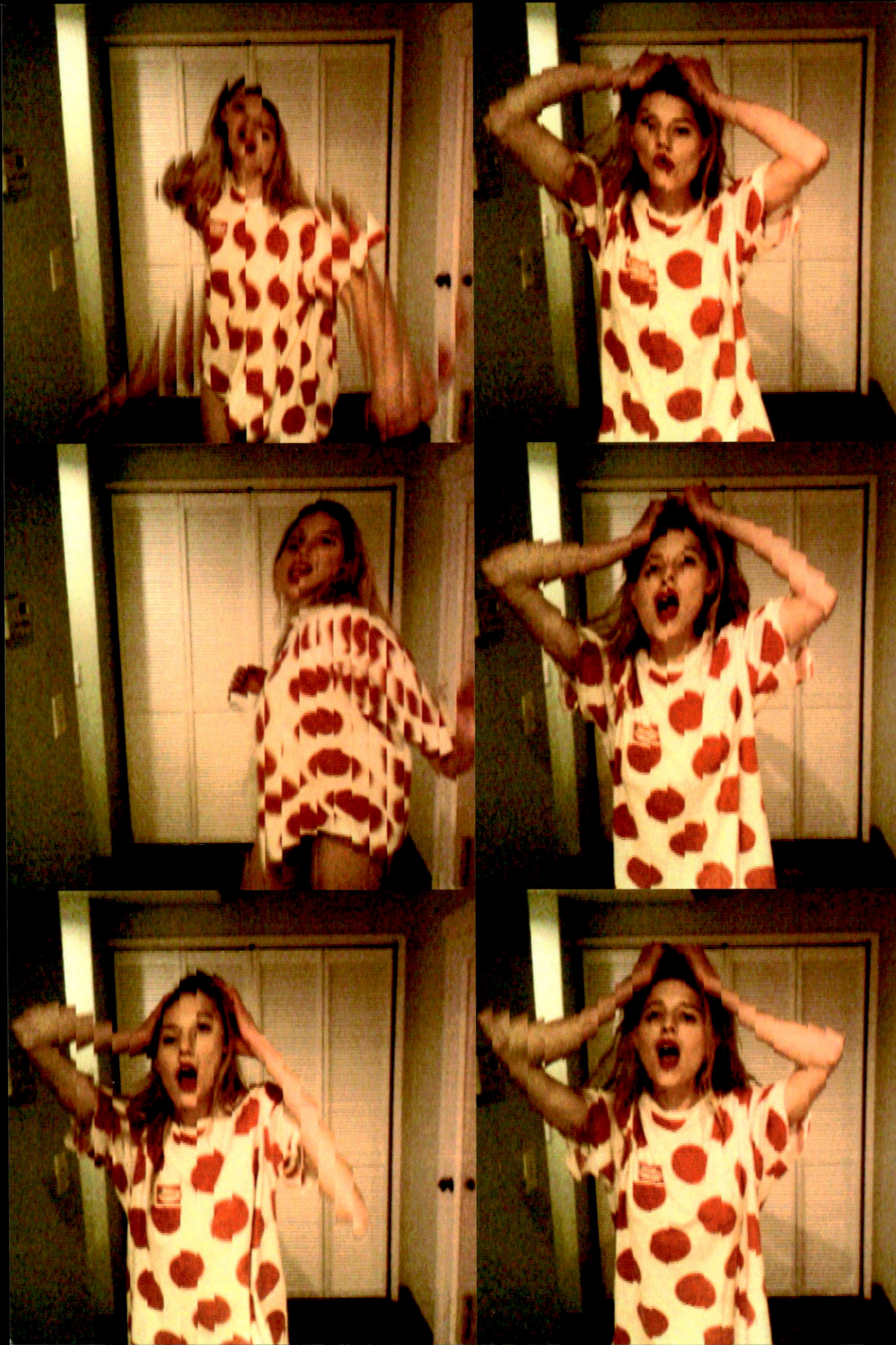

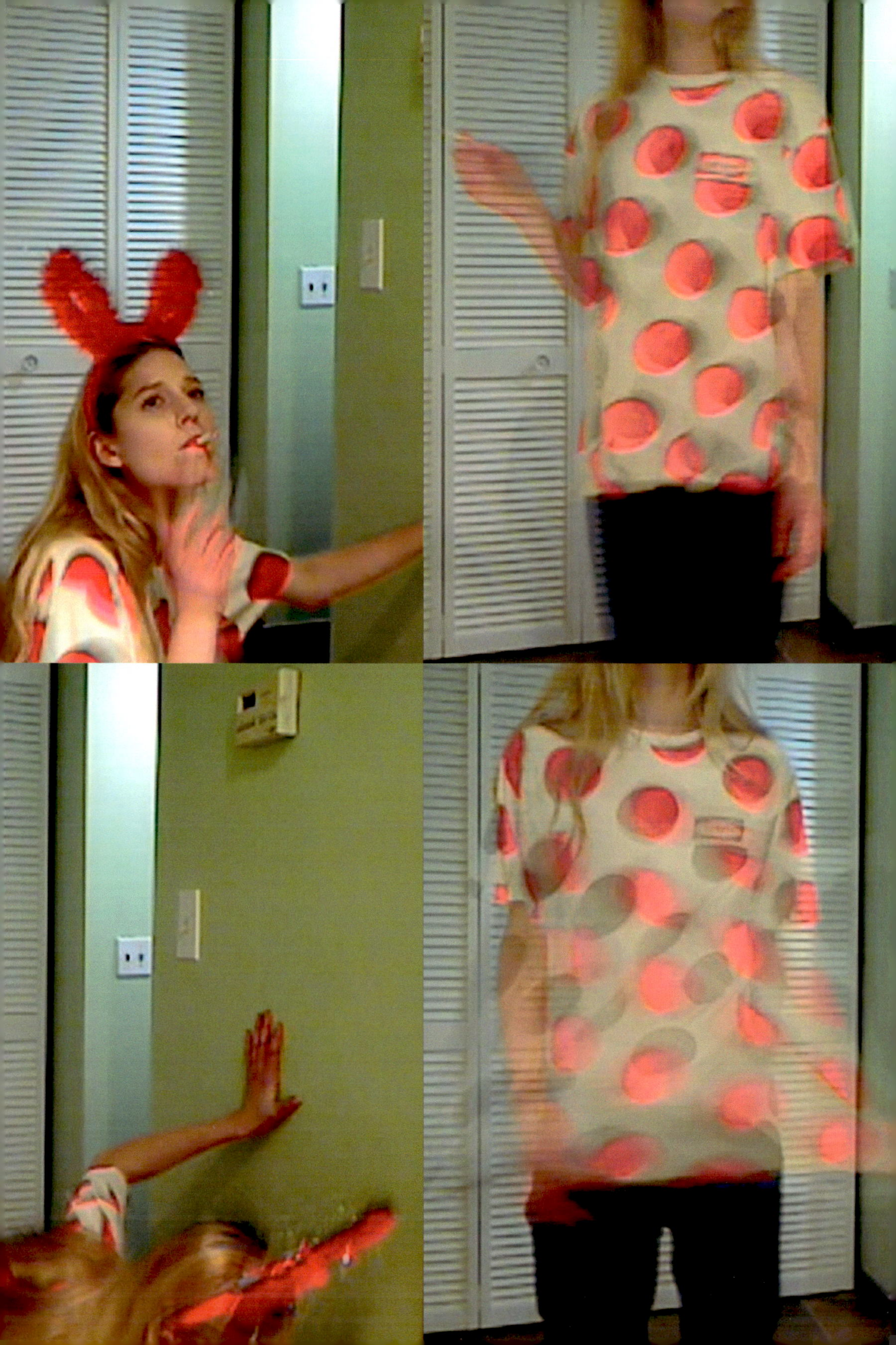

FOR ALL THE GIRLS—IT'S NEVER TOO LATE TO LOG OFF

Selected Video Stills, 2011–2018

ISBN 978-1-948434-10-2

Published by Hesse Press, Los Angeles, California. Designed by John Wiese.
© 2021 Hesse Press, LLC.